RICH OLIVER'S
Monday Morning
PEP TALK

Rich Oliver's Monday Morning Pep Talk

(c) 2014

Papa Rich Press

1529 Eureka Road Suite 110
Roseville, CA 95661
(916)-365-6609

All rights reserved. No part of this book may be reproduced, stored in a retrieval system, or transmitted by any means, electronic, mechanical, photocopying, recording or otherwise, without written permission from the author.

Index

Getting Started 8

Created in God's Image 16
   Introduction 16
   A Heart for Your Generation 18
   You are Called by God 21
   A Great Day to be Filled with Courage 24
   He First Loved Us 28
   I Want My Inheritance 31
   The Importance of Being Created in
      God's Image 34
   You are a Champion 37
   You are Blessed! 40

Living in His Authority 44
   Introduction 44
   Our Authority in Prayer 47
   Benefits of Empowerment 49
   Courage Takes Action 52
   Fear Not! 54
   Are You Free... Enough? 57
   Prayer for Finances 60
   Winners and Champions 63
   You Want to Go Deeper? 66

Living a Hope-Filled Life 70
   Introduction 70
   He Will Do What is Best... For You 73
   When You Feel Lost 75
   Breaking off Doubt 78
   God's Favor is Lavish 80
   Stop Being a Victim 84
   Give God Praise 88
   Keeping Me Safe 91
   You Win! 95

It's a New Day 98
   Introduction 98
   Finding God 100
   Benefits of Empowerment 103
   Should'a, Could'a, Would'a 106
   It's a New Season! 109
   A Great Day to Daydream! 112
   Today is Your Day! 115
   A New Outlook on Life 117
   A Season of Harvest 121

Living with Great Joy! 124
   Introduction 124
   Do Real Christians Laugh? 127
   Focus On Your Blessings 129
   Hold Tightly To Your Joy 132
   Joy of the Lord 136
   I Love To Laugh! 140
   You're So Special! 143
   Enjoy Life! 146

Living a Blessed Life 149
   Introduction 149
   Religion Vs. Relationship 151
   The Power of Blessing 154
   What Do You Speak? 157
   Genuine Relationships 160
   Blessing Others 163
   When We Fall 166
   You Are Blessed! 170

Living Through the Holidays 173
   New Year's Day 173
   Groundhog Day 176
   Valentine's Day 180
   Easter 183
   Independence Day 186
   Halloween 189
   Election Day 192
   Thanksgiving Day 195
   Christmas Eve 197
   Christmas Day 200
   Happy Birthday! 203
   Happy Anniversary 206

ACKNOWLEDGEMENTS

A Big THANK YOU to Eric Leach, my son Kyle, and my wonderful wife Lindy for their editorial oversight and long hours in correcting my run-on sentences and poor grammar.

Also, a special thanks to Kyle Oliver and Suzette Allen for all the work on the cover; their creative input made this book a reality! And thanks to Christina Files, who helped with editing and publishing.

You are all loved and appreciated.

Suzette Allen can be reached at
www.suzetteallen.com

Christina Files can be reached at
www.christinafiles.com

DEDICATION

I dedicate this book to my best friend,
my partner, and my wife Lindy.
In a life of learning and discovery,
her Spirit-filled passion,
humility and humor has
brought me through the trials of this life.

I also dedicate this to my three sons,
Rich, Matt and Kyle,
who have spontaneously taught me about
myself and my desperate need
for God's Grace.

ENDORSEMENTS

Since I was little I have always said that my father was my favorite preacher. As a Pastors Kid (P.K.) we were at church a lot and it took a lot to capture and keep my attention. My dad, with his passion, humor and his love and knowledge of the Word of God could always captivate me and inspire me in my walk with God. Now as a senior pastor, I am still encouraged by his daily revelations. His clever humor and spiritual insights are refreshing and stirring. His powerful new book "Monday Morning Pep Talks" gives you a daily dose of heavenly insights to start your day off right. I am blessed that now everyone gets to experience what I have been enjoying for years from my father: the lighthearted way that he brings life-changing words. This is not a book you read once and set down; this is a book that can encourage you year after year after year.

Pastor Matthew Oliver
Senior Pastor, The Family Church
Author, *Taking Back the Night*

Rich Oliver has a common man's way of communicating uncommon truth. As you read through Rich's musings, you may, as I have, catch yourself thinking "I know that," while realizing that you now know it all over again in a fresh way. It's like finding treasure in another man's field, treasure worth the price. Having received Rich's *Monday Morning Pep Talk* by email for several years, I was excited to see him put them in print so others can profit from them.

David Crone
Senior Leader of The Mission
Author of *Decisions that Define Us*,
The Power of Your Life Message,
and *Declarations that Empower Us*

Rich is so appropriately named. Rich is Rich and Rich is rich. He is true to himself and proven to be true to his God; hence, the Lord has made him rich in truth, in experience, in humor, and in wisdom. In reading this book you will share in all of those ways. Lindy is his perfect match: loving, honest, and always encouraging. That's the way I know them and why I highly recommend "Monday Morning Pep Talk" by Rich Oliver.

> Pastor Robin McMillan
> Queen City Church, Charlotte, NC
> Former Senior Pastor of Morning Star Fellowship Church in Fort Mill, South Carolina for the 10 years and author of
> *Mystic Moosetales*

Richard brings strength, wisdom, timely insight, revelation and encouragement to pastors and leaders all over the world. Just recently I encountered a pastor in ministry who called me and told me that after meeting with Richard he finally felt for the first time that he had found his spiritual father. That is the type of impact Richard has on those around him and those he influences. Every time I encounter Rich, I leave encouraged and strengthened and I believe that "Monday Morning Pep Talk" will do the same for you.

> Banning Liebscher
> Director of Jesus Culture
> Sacramento, CA

Getting Started...

THIS SHOULD PEP YOU UP: GOD IS YOUR BIGGEST FAN

When the Lord began talking to me about writing and sharing a Monday Morning Pep Talk, it was as simple as it sounds: beginning the week, or any day of the week, with an encouraging word directed by the Holy Spirit.

The truth is, I needed to dig in and find a good word to begin my week. So at first, the "Pep Talk," was just for me and then for Lindy. Then I began to send it out to some friends and then to Facebook. And now, finally, I decided to share with... well, with YOU!

By the way, I am not a writer. I am a speaker who writes like I speak. I am fairly funny, a little sarcastic and getting older. I have instructed my wonderful editors to leave my ramblings pretty much as they are: fresh, raw and loving.

I have the "Pep Talks" divided into seven topical sections to help you if you find yourself in a particular area of need. I have also included a section for holidays. In case you were wondering, I did NOT neglect Groundhog Day. I know... amazing!

I have included some of my favorite humorous (at least I hope they are) one-liners (at least I hope they are). I actually believe Christians need to laugh A LOT... and then laugh A LOT MORE!!!

So as you prepare to read *Monday Morning Pep Talk*, allow me to encourage you with the following scriptures and thoughts.

God has given you the ability to be a champion in your life, right now, wherever you find yourself. Today you can reign with Him over all things. There is nothing too difficult for you. As you look to God your possibilities in life are without limitation.

- In Luke 18:27 Jesus said, *"What is impossible with men is possible with God."*
- Philippians 4:13 states, *"I can do all things through Him who gives me strength."*
- Romans 8:37 declares, *"No, in all these things we are more than conquerors through Him who loved us."*

Today, in this special introduction, I am declaring over you what God says you can do in partnership with Him. I encourage you to receive this "Pep Talk!"

Grab it – Believe it

Have great belief in what Jesus says concerning your position with Him and what He can do in and through you!

Hebrews 11:6 reminds us, *"And without faith it is impossible to please God, because anyone who comes to Him must believe that He exists and that He rewards those who earnestly seek Him."*

Mark 9:23-24 *"'If you can'?" Jesus said "Everything is possible for one who believes." Immediately the boy's father exclaimed, "I do believe; help me overcome my unbelief!"*

- Today, do you believe that God has made you equal to any task that He gives you?
- Today, do you believe that God will take your impossibilities and turn them into possibilities?
- Today, do you believe that you are more than a conqueror through Him?
- Today, do you believe you are a champion for Christ?

Getting Started...

Ephesians 1:19-20... *"and what is His incomparably great power for us who believe. That power is the same as the mighty strength He exerted when He raised Christ from the dead and seated Him at His right hand in the heavenly realms."*

You can change

Are you willing to go through the changes of being conformed into the image of Jesus Christ? Our life in Christ consists of yielding ourselves to His transforming grace.

Second Corinthians 3:18 encourages us, *"And we all, who with unveiled faces contemplate the Lord's glory, are being transformed into His image with ever-increasing glory, which comes from the Lord, who is the Spirit."*

Today and every day you are putting on the new man who is created after Jesus Christ!

Ephesians 4:22-24 reminds us... *"You were taught, with regard to your former way of life, to put off your old self, which is being corrupted by its deceitful desires; to be made new in the attitude of your minds; and to put on the new self, created to be like God in true righteousness and holiness."*

You are loved by God – You can love others

One of the key ingredients in becoming a champion for Christ is being able to fully receive His love into your life! This gives you the freedom to grow and learn to be a blessing and to love others.

Romans 5:5 *"And hope does not put us to shame, because God's love has been poured out into our hearts through the Holy Spirit, who has been given to us."*

In John 13:34 Jesus advises, *"A new command I give you: Love one another. As I have loved you, so you must love one another."*

Getting Started...

In First John 3:16 we are taught,

"This is how we know what love is: Jesus Christ laid down His life for us. And we ought to lay down our lives for our Brothers and sisters."

You make a difference

Remember, you have been sent into this world to be salt and light. When you are doing the things that glorify God, you are able to make a difference in the world! You have been given to this generation to serve the purpose of God.

Esther 4:14 notes, *"For if you remain silent at this time, relief and deliverance for the Jews will arise from another place, but you and your father's family will perish. And who knows but that you have come to your royal position for such a time as this?"*

You will continue to accomplish great things.

In John 14:12 we are assured, *"Very truly I tell you, whoever believes in Me will do the works I have been doing, and they will do even greater things than these, because I am going to the Father."*

Have you even begun to dream what those *"greater things"* might look like through your life?

You are a finisher.

Second Timothy 4:6-7 shares, *"For I am already being poured out as a drink offering, and the time of my departure is at hand. I have fought the good fight, I have finished the race, I have kept the faith."*

Each and every day, remember God's desire toward you is for you to become a great champion for Christ. As you continue to live your life by the revelation and power of the Holy Spirit, you need to stand on the truth that you are the great champion that Christ has made you to be!

Getting Started...

God is taking you into a season where you are going to have such great influence and impact, it is ridiculous. Those seeds you have sown have not been wasted. The fields are ripe for harvest!

You are going to like this

Today I declare over you, In His name: new avenues, new doors, God's best! No matter what! No turning back!

Psalm 100 declares, *"Shout for joy to the Lord, all the earth. Worship the Lord with gladness; come before Him with joyful songs. Know that the Lord is God. It is He who made us, and we are His; We are His people, the sheep of His pasture. Enter His gates with thanksgiving and His courts with praise; give thanks to Him and praise His name. For the Lord is good and His love endures forever; His faithfulness continues through all generations."*

Today

I pray that you will know the grace and peace of our Lord Jesus Christ and be totally encouraged by the HOLY SPIRIT.

I declare that His Holy Spirit will both overshadow and consume you.

I pray that you be filled with strength, courage and focus in everything you do.

I declare the blessings of Heaven over you, your family, and your ministry.

Colossians 1: 11-12 *"Being strengthened with all power according to His glorious might so that you may have great endurance and patience, and giving joyful thanks to the Father, who has qualified you to share in the inheritance of His holy people in the kingdom of light."*

Getting Started...

I want you to know today that you are amazing. You may not feel amazing, but you can't trust your feelings anyway. After all, it's God's that count. Accept what God says about you, agree with Him that it is true of you and become the spiritual person you are.

Knowing who you are in Jesus is a key to a successful Christian life .

Your identity doesn't depend on something you do or have done. Your true identity is who you are in Christ.

Please stop living out of who other people say you are and take hold of the truth of God's word. Find out what God says about you and agree with Him.

- I am loved (1 John 3:3)
- I am accepted (Ephesians 1:6)
- I am a child of God (John 1:12)
- I am Jesus' friend (John 15:14)
- I am a joint heir with Jesus, sharing His inheritance with Him (Romans 8:17)
- I am united with God and one spirit with Him (1 Corinthians 6:17)
- I am a temple of God. His spirit and His life live in me (1 Corinthians 6:19)
- I am a member of Christ's body. (1 Corinthians 2:27)
- I am a Saint (Ephesians 1:1)
- I am redeemed and forgiven (Colossians 1:14)
- I am complete in Jesus Christ (Colossians 2:10)
- I am free from condemnation (Romans 8:1)
- I am a new creation because I am in Christ (2 Corinthians 5:17)
- I am chosen of God, holy and dearly loved (Colossians 3:12)

Getting Started...

- I am established, anointed, and sealed by God (2 Corinthians 1:21)
- I do not have a spirit of fear, but of love, power, and a sound mind (2 Timothy 1:7)
- I am God's co-worker (2 Corinthians 6:1)
- I am seated in heavenly places with Christ (Ephesians 2:6)
- I have direct access to God (Ephesians 2:18)
- I am chosen to bear fruit (John 15:16)
- I am one of God's living stones, being built up in Christ as a spiritual house (1 Peter 2:5)
- I have been given exceedingly great and precious promises by God by which I share His nature (2 Peter 1:4)
- I can always know the presence of God because He never leaves me (Hebrews 13:5)
- God works in me to help me do the things He wants me to do (Philippians 2:13)
- I can ask God for wisdom and He will give me what I need (James 1:5)

Simply choose to believe what God says about you. Each of the following "Pep Talks" will help you to do just that.

I would love to hear your thoughts, your ideas or questions as you read these "Pep Talks." I invite you to e-mail me at peptalk888@msn.com or friend me on Facebook at familychurchfather@facebook.com.

I pray you are ENCOURAGED today!

Rich Oliver

Created in God's Image
INTRODUCTION

I regularly enjoy a middle of the night "Papa and me" time. Most often, He speaks to me about His love for me and for you! Love is a powerful thing, especially the love of our Father God, which is the greatest love of all.

He loves us unconditionally. When others reject us, He loves us. When we don't love ourselves, He loves us. After all, we are created in God's own image. I believe that receiving a true revelation of how much He delights in us and cares for us is liberating. It frees us from trying to win or earn what is already ours.

Recognizing our worth and value to God is the thing that combats the enemy's attempts to lower our sense of self-worth, esteem, and worthiness. Simply put, to know God's love is to know your worth.

The Holy Spirit directed me to Ephesians 3:17-19. It says, *"And I pray that you, being rooted and established in love, may have power, together with all the Lord's holy people, to grasp how wide and long and high and deep is the love of Christ, and to know this love that surpasses knowledge – that you may be filled to the measure of all the fullness of God."*

I pray you will receive divine revelation of God's love and experience the fullness of the Holy Spirit. As a result of knowing Him in His fullness, you will be empowered to see, believe, be, and do all He has written into your heart.

When you enjoy the security of His love, you will know without a doubt you are equipped, capable, and chosen.

Enjoy this section on "Created in God's Image," because you are!!! Allow me to speak the following over you:

Introduction

- Be blessed with God's supernatural wisdom and clear direction for life.
- Be blessed with creativity, courage, ability and abundance.
- Be blessed with a great family, good friends and good health.
- Be blessed with faith, favor and fulfillment.
- Be blessed with success, supernatural strength, promotion and divine protection.
- Be blessed with an obedient heart and a positive outlook on life.
- Be blessed in your community when you go in and when you come out.
- May every negative word that has ever been spoken over you be broken right now.
- Everything you put your hand to will prosper and succeed.

Be blessed in Jesus' Name.

> **So today is the tomorrow you worried about yesterday**

A HEART FOR YOUR GENERATION

Two things that matter:
Our relationship with God and our responsibility towards man.

These two things every person should care about above all else: his relationship with God and how he has lived and operated within his generation.

We should be those who live according to God's heart and thus serve our generation. We should not merely care for our own things. Too many people just plan for themselves, or else they serve their generation in a manner that is not according to God's heart. Far too many Christians have their own plans and simply seek to go their own way. Yet, many people in the Bible demonstrated a life impacted by God in every area, not just "church life," but trusted that God was able to take care of them.

Today, God is still looking for those who would be passionate for Him and His Kingdom. God is asking this generation, "Do you care about what is on My heart?"

As Spirit-filled people, we should have a heart like King David, who had a heart after God's own heart. David pursued the heart of God and we should follow his example by pursuing the heart of God in our lives and in our generation. The Bible said that David served his own generation and was buried among the forefathers (Acts 13:36).

What a powerful statement: David served the purposes of God in his generation! God is searching for people who will serve His eternal purposes in the earth. Even Jesus said that He did not come to be served but to serve (Matthew 20:28).

The Holy Spirit is speaking to us today about impacting the generations. I am so excited to be learning the principle of serving my generation as well as generations to come. I believe wholeheartedly that David did not want to die among the forefathers until the purposes of God were fulfilled in his generation.

I don't think any of us should allow ourselves to sit around acting "dead." I want the Lord's destiny for my life and I want to see the will of the Lord done. I believe it is not the will of the Father that a generation dies prematurely and aborts their divine assignment and purpose in the earth.

God desires for you and I to live abundantly in His spiritual kingdom on earth and finish the work that He has entrusted to us. Jesus finished the work that He was sent to finish and fulfill. And in John 4:34, Jesus explained: *"My food...is to do the will of Him who sent Me and to finish His work."* Moreover, David prepared, blessed and imparted the heavenly patterns and visions of God to the next generation (his son, Solomon).

Importantly, it should be the heart of any believer to reveal the plans and purposes of God to both their generation and the generation to come. We must be passionate about their success.

PRAYER POINT

Dear Heavenly Father, You wrote a book of all our days before we were even born. How awesome You are, Father. You have dreamed a dream for me and for everyone, and written a novel of our days.

I declare this generation will fulfill their dreamed destiny. I declare that there is a generation that is marked by spiritual violence, by extreme passion, sacrifice and devotion. I pray this generation will seize the moment and turn nations back to God (Matthew 11:12).

Lord, I declare this is a generation who will wrestle with You in the midst of darkness and will not give up or give in until they see You face to face and receive your blessing (Psalm 24:6).

> My question is this — Why does the sound of the recliner opening always remind Lindy that the trash needs to be taken out?

YOU ARE CALLED BY GOD

You Are Valuable To God

God loves you and you are very valuable to Him. Unfortunately, many people don't realize this and feel worthless, thinking that God can't value them.

You Have A Great Purpose and Destiny

God has a great plan for your life. You are not here by accident, but you have a call on your life. The call that God has given you is unique: no one will ever do exactly what God has called you to do. We Christians are all invaluable parts of Christ's body and each part is necessary to get the whole body to work (1 Corinthians 12:12-27). In the same way as the body has many different parts with unique functions, we are different and unique too. It's no accident that God has made us different! We are intentionally different so that we can complement each other. We are all unique and just as valuable; no one is more or less valuable than one other. Everyone is valuable and everyone has something to contribute. Everyone is needed in the kingdom of God.

When the Lord called Gideon to deliver the Israelites, Gideon felt so worthless that he was skeptical that the Lord would choose him to bring deliverance to his people. He balked at even considering that the Lord would favor him. Gideon's insecurity led him to test God several times with a fleece (Judges 6).

Yet God went along with Gideon's tests. He assured Gideon that He was working with him. Once Gideon started acting on God's call, you never saw

Gideon wavering again. What you did see was the miraculous working of the Lord through Gideon's hands.

Many of us have heard the call of the Lord ourselves. We've tried to question whether God really wanted to use us. We've tried to offer up our own little "tests" to prove that God is really with us.

Now is the time for us to move past the questioning stage. It's time for us to actually step out in faith!

Is there anyone still hiding in fear in the winepress, like Gideon. Are you missing out on experiencing miracles because you're too afraid to step out in faith? Don't miss out on your destiny because of fear! God may have called you to do something so extraordinary, unheard of, and peculiar; but if God's asking you to do it, you can't expect anything but miraculous results!

Your life is supposed to be full of God's glory. As you respond in faith to what God is asking, His glory will shine through for all to see! You have been called to live a life of miracles!

(Judges 6:12-16) *[12]"When the angel of the Lord appeared to Gideon, he said, "The Lord is with you, mighty warrior." [13]"Pardon me, my lord," Gideon replied, "but if the Lord is with us, why has all this happened to us? Where are all his wonders that our ancestors told us about when they said, 'Did not the Lord bring us up out of Egypt?' But now the Lord has abandoned us and given us into the hand of Midian." [14]The Lord turned to him and said, "Go in the strength you have and save Israel out of Midian's hand. Am I not sending you?" [15]"Pardon me, my lord," Gideon replied, "but how can I save Israel? My clan is the weakest in Manasseh, and I am the least in my family."*

^{16}The Lord answered, "I will be with you, and you will strike down all the Midianites, leaving none alive."

PRAYER POINT

Father in heaven, I worship You with my words, with my heart and with my obedient living. Fill me anew with Your Holy Spirit so that I can fulfill the highest destiny You have for me. Give me wisdom, humility and courage. As I continue to pray, let Your answers strengthen my faith and prepare me for a life of miracles that will change and bless this world.

May I continue to grow in You Lord, to love and serve others, and to be Your instrument of blessing to those around me. In Jesus' name. Amen.

> If anyone ever tells you your dreams are silly, remember there's a millionaire walking around that invented the pool noodle.

A GREAT DAY TO BE FILLED WITH COURAGE

Dare: An act of daring, to have courage, a challenge.

Have you ever been given a dare to do something great? Great accomplishments take great courage.

What challenges are you facing this week? We live in a culture that wants us to conform, but we are called by Christ to be different.

We were never meant to live in a world like the one we are living in. You were not created to live in a world that has the presence of sin, injustice, wrongdoing and evil. That was never God's intention for you. Yet we feel this pressure to conform to this world around us.

Daniel has some great advice on how to rise above the ordinary in this world and how to live a holy life in this society. Daniel knew who he was. If we want to dare to be different in a world that wants us to conform, then we must settle in our minds, once and for all, just who we are.

- Self-Esteem: it seems Daniel had a balanced self-esteem. Daniel knew what he was worth and his incredible value in God's eyes—this shaped his behavior.
- Self-respect: Daniel had a healthy self-respect for his body. The Bible encourages healthy living and care for the body.
- Self-confidence: Daniel had a solid self-confidence, showing that he had surrendered his intellect to the Lord as well. Talking about Daniel and his friends, we read: "In every matter of wisdom and understanding about which the king questioned them, he found them

ten times better than all the magicians and enchanters in his whole kingdom" (Daniel 1:20).

- Another truth is that Daniel knew why he was there. If you want to dare to be different in a world that wants you to conform, then you must settle in your mind, once and for all, just why you are here—this place, this moment, these circumstances.

- Daniel lived his life for an audience of one—his Lord. Daniel has a vision of the glorified Jesus; in this vision, Jesus says to him: *"Do not be afraid, Daniel. Since the first day that you set your mind to gain understanding and to humble yourself before your God, your words were heard, and I have come in response to them"* (Daniel 10:12).

- Daniel wasn't easily distracted from his life's purpose. He refused to "perform" spiritual gifts for any reward. Under great pressure, Daniel showed that wealth and power were no distraction to him. Once king Nebachadnezzar offered Daniel payment to interpret some writings, Daniel responded: "You may keep your gifts for yourself and give your rewards to someone else. Nevertheless, I will read the writing for the king and tell him what it means (Daniel 5:17). The Lord has a purpose for your life too—and His opinion of the way you live and invest your life is the only opinion that really matters.

- Daniel knew where his strength came from. Daniel is famous for being a man of prayer. It's clear that Daniel looked to the Lord as his source of strength to live the sacred life in a challenging society.

- Daniel prayed even though it was difficult. When Daniel learned that the decree against prayer to the Lord had been published, he went home to his upstairs room where the windows opened toward Jerusalem. Three times a day he got down on his knees and prayed, giving thanks to his God, just as he had done before (Daniel 6:10). Although the expression of his faith was forbidden, he persisted with it.

- Daniel's prayers were answered.
"…*your words were heard, and I have come in response to them*" (Daniel 10:12).

As a result:

- He was protected in adversity (Daniel 6:21-22).
- He received insight into God's will (Daniel 9:22).
- He was given patience even when things weren't clear (Daniel 12:8-9, 13).

Jesus was similar to Daniel in many ways. Jesus knew who He was, why He was here and where His strength came from. Jesus had the ability to live a life that didn't conform to the religious, cultural or political world around Him — because of the power of the Holy Spirit in us, we can do the same.

Do you want some great news? You are created in God's image. He's written his plan and purpose right into your DNA. He has given you the Holy Spirit; as a result, you are filled with courage. You naturally gravitate toward the gifts and calling you were designed for.

The enemy doesn't want you to find your life and purpose in Christ. He wants you to conform to this world and forget about your dreams and destiny. But like a good earthly father, your Heavenly Father wants you to discover what you were created for and to pursue the passions of your heart. The Holy Spirit will strengthen and encourage you to boldly and confidently step out in faith.

You see, you are created in God's image. You have a destiny to be a world-changer. Choose it.

PRAYER POINT

Almighty God, Who gives strength to the weak and upholds those who might fall, give me courage to do what is right, for those that trust in You have no need to fear. Make me brave to face any danger which may now threaten me. Give me the help that You have promised to those who ask it, that I may overcome my fears and go bravely forward. Because I am filled with Your Holy Spirit, I am also full of courage. Nothing You have called me to do will be too hard for me.

Right now, I place my trust in Your power and goodness. Thank you my Lord, Amen.

> This morning during my sermon I have decided that if I can't convince them, I can at least confuse them!!

HE FIRST LOVED US

"We love Him because He first loved us." (1 John 4:19)

This verse is key to the healing of the broken heart. The fulfillment of your human nature and the true meaning of your life is found in God's love. The only way to have a truly satisfying relationship is here.

"Then God said, 'Let Us make mankind in Our image, in Our likeness, so that they may rule over the fish in the sea and the birds in the sky, over the livestock and all the wild animals, and over all the creatures that move along the ground.' So God created mankind in His own image, in the image of God He created them; male and female He created them." (Genesis 1:26-27)

Did you know that you were created for love? The Bible says that you were created by God in His image and likeness. That means many things. Your life has great value. God made you; therefore, you are not junk. You are not an accident. You are not second class. Instead, you are valuable and precious to God. Your life has meaning and purpose. God has a great plan for you. More importantly, it means you were created for love.

First John 4:8 and First John 4:16 tell us "God is love."

If God is love, and He created you in His image, then it makes sense that you were created for love. God's purpose in creating you was that He might love you and that you might love Him back. Your heart was designed to receive love and to give love, first with God, then with others. If you are not fulfilling your purpose and your design, you will never be truly satisfied as a human being.

By design, every person, before he or she is damaged in this broken world, has the desire to be loved and to love in return. Where did we get this yearning? From God Himself! God also has the desire to love and be loved. Love, by its very nature, wants to draw close, to give and express itself in goodness, kindness, and all the fruit of the Spirit (Galatians 5:22-23).

What God wants most is to have a loving and intimate relationship with you. He did not create you to be a servant, yet those who love Him gladly serve Him. He did not create you just to "do His will," although love compels one to do His will. He created you to satisfy the desire and yearning of own His heart: He created you to love you and to receive love from you in return.

God created the world with a command from His mouth. He can create anything He wants with one spoken word. Yet, there is one thing our all-powerful God chose not create by command: a love relationship. Love forced or programmed into us would not be authentic or satisfying. Instead, it would be a sham, a meaningless counterfeit.

God demonstrates His love to us (Romans 5:8). He expresses His love to us. He seeks to draw us to Himself (Jeremiah 31:3). He never forces His love on us. God wants an authentic love relationship with you, and He is willing to be the one to love you first.

PRAYER POINT

Father God, I come into Your presence so aware of my human frailty, yet overwhelmed by Your love for me. I thank You that there is no human experience I might walk through where Your love cannot reach me. If I climb the highest mountain You are there. If I find myself in the darkest valley of my life, You are there. Teach me today to love You more. Help me to rest in the love that asks nothing more than the simple trusting heart of a child.

In Jesus name, Amen.

> Anyone else experience that awkward moment when you set something down for a second and it disappears off the face of the earth?

I WANT MY INHERITANCE!

Everyone wants their inheritance, especially if it is of considerable value to them. As part of your spiritual inheritance, you have the favor of God, which has greater benefit to you than any natural inheritance you could receive. The favor of God brings God's ability, God's empowerment, God's anointing, God's help, and God's power. Plain and simple—when God is involved in your affairs, there is an increase in favor, leading to a more productive and fruitful life.

Operating in your inheritance will eliminate the red tape of mere men that causes you heartache and headaches. Your birthright gives you promotions and blessings you could never expect in the natural. In this season, walking in your inheritance is not just beneficial, it is essential.

With God's favor in your life, you reign as a king instead of being ruled by negative circumstances. Let me give you some good news right now about the favor of God—this is the set time for God to favor you! How do I know? Favor is part of your redemptive package, purchased by the finished work of Christ. The nature of your loving Heavenly Father is to lavish His favor on you—especially when things are tough, difficult, or seemingly impossible with no natural way out.

We are reminded of this in Psalm 102:13 when it says, *"You will arise and have compassion on Zion, for it is time to show favor to her; the appointed time has come."*

As a child of God, you should never rule out the favor of God in the affairs of your life. Instead, continually look for and expect God's intervention. Be aware of His goodness at all times, especially in the most difficult situations. The Lord loves to pass on His blessing during hardship. When favor comes, be sure to immediately thank Him and acknowledge Him saying, "That's the favor of God!" Why? Because every time you acknowledge God's favor coming to you, more faith arises in you to receive an increase of His good will.

The favor of God has the potential to change every negative aspect of your life. Favor is a spiritual law. Just as you can expect the law of gravity to work when you need it, you can count on the favor of God to bring you out of the most difficult situations. I am telling you, in your worst situation, when you have the most insurmountable difficulties in your life, you can set your hope wholly, completely, unchangeably on the favor of God.

Paul confirms this in Second Corinthians 12:9, when he says, *"But he said to me, 'My grace* [My favor and lovingkindness and mercy] *is sufficient for you* [sufficient against any danger and enables you to bear the trouble manfully], *for my power is made perfect* [fulfilled and completed] *in weakness.' Therefore I will boast all the more gladly about my weaknesses, so that Christ's power may rest on me."*

Think about how an inheritance comes to us from our parents. Does one work for it? No, for then it would be wages. The parents have done all the work. They save up, and then upon their death, they leave a gift. All one needs to do is keep rightly related to the parents and the inheritance is theirs. Similarly, in the spiritual realm all the work has been done by Christ. The Father wants to bestow an inheritance on us. It becomes ours when we are rightly related to the Father through Jesus Christ. Are you qualified? God's word says if you are in Christ, you are able to receive all the riches promised to the children of God.

PRAYER POINT

Father, thank You for the inheritance I have in Christ. I want to own these blessings and make them a part of my daily life. I thank You for the favor that is my inheritance. I ask You now, Lord, to equip me with the supernatural gifts of the Holy Spirit listed in First Corinthians 12. I yield my will to You, Father, one hundred per cent, and ask You now to release into my life all the gifts You desire for me that I may better serve You.

I thank You God for forgiving me of my sins and for making me clean. I thank You for Your anointing and empowering. I promise to give You all the glory for the miracles You work through me. I receive this empowerment and inheritance by faith and thank You for manifesting these supernatural gifts in my life, as You choose.

I pray this in the name of Jesus Christ, Amen!

> Sex education should require them to listen to a crying baby for five hours and to watch the same episode of Barney over and over again!

THE IMPORTANCE OF BEING CREATED IN GOD'S IMAGE

"And we all, who with unveiled faces contemplate the Lord's glory, are being transformed into His image with ever-increasing glory, which comes from the Lord, who is the Spirit." (Second Corinthians 3:18)

Do you ever look in the mirror and wish you were different? Maybe you are too short, or too tall, or too thin, or too heavy. The list never seems to end. Even the super model seems to be preoccupied with the one slight imperfection that nobody else even notices. It seems that most of us, in varying degrees, are not happy with the way we were made.

For some of us, it might be dissatisfaction with our appearance; while for others it might be that we're not smart enough, or outgoing enough, or so on. Our culture has believed a lie that says we have to look and act a certain way in order to be accepted or valued. Even those who make up the standards of acceptance feel unaccepted deep down in their hearts. No matter how hard we try to change ourselves inside or out in order to gain love and acceptance, it will always elude us.

Often when we read those first chapters of Genesis, we think of being created in God's physical image and leave it right there. If so, we are really missing the most important part. The Hebrews have an important word that goes with that story of creation: it is called "Neshama" — the human soul. They believed it was not the physical image that was so important. But rather, "Neshama," the human soul that God placed in us, that is the vital imprint of His image.

It is important to take a deeper look at the fact that our value of being made in God's image is not merely based on the physical aspect of who we are. More than that, we are uniquely created in God's image with a human soul. As human beings, we can be born again allowing the Holy Spirit to live within us.

If we say we are made in God's likeness, then God must be short, tall, fat, skinny, attractive, not attractive, with all the physical perfections and imperfections common to humanity.

However, if what makes us like our Father is something within and not merely two arms and legs, two hands and feet, a torso, neck and head, then we are moving beyond mere physical importance relating to what places us within His image. Then, we can truly see the worth of each individual beyond the material boundaries—your worth to our Lord.

Having been made in God's image, the core of our being has been given the ability to reason, to be self-aware, to practice free will, to choose and act on love.

Because we have a human soul, we can distinguish right from wrong—we begin to see the importance of life issues. We understand why it matters that babies are not destroyed and why it matters that the elderly are not discarded, for we are dealing with human souls made in God's image, carrying about the human soul implanted by God. For those who have accepted Christ, they carry the very Spirit of God within.

What all this means to Christians with afflictions and disabilities is that our value and worth is not dependent upon functioning limbs, or working eyes and ears, or even healthy brains, but upon the fact that we are God's children given a human soul and are recipients of the Spirit of God. By our very existence, we matter.

We are representatives of God on earth as He lives, moves, and breathes through our lives. God makes us valuable. God makes our lives worthwhile. God can impact the world through us, not because we are examples of physical perfection, but because we are human souls carrying about the love of God within us.

We matter because He matters. It is a privilege and an honor to be God's children. We matter because we matter to Him.

Your life has value because God has given you life. Don't let physical disabilities or limitations get you down. Hold your head high, because you are a living example of the image of God.

PRAYER POINT

Dear Lord, sometimes we are discouraged because of physical disabilities and limitations. But do not let us lose sight that we are made in Your image, and we praise You for it.

Forgive me for not agreeing with You that I am fearfully and wonderfully made. Forgive me for believing the lies that I have to be somebody other than who I am. Help me to come into agreement with Your love for me and not despise all my imperfections. The fact that You love me and accept me is more important than love and acceptance from anyone else.

I am thankful that I am Your child, and that I am fearfully and wonderfully made! I know that full well. I pray these things in the name of Your beloved Son Jesus, Amen.

YOU ARE A CHAMPION

This is a great everyday truth — you and I are champions! It is so good to know that we are winners. No matter how the situation may look, we are already assured of victory because we know Jesus Christ and are filled with the Holy Spirit. All we have to do is stand strong in Him. We are Champions!

The Holy Spirit has been revealing new dreams that we need to pursue. The "old us" would be a bit apprehensive about starting down some of these paths. However, the "new us" is excited! Any opposition or need is already taken care of by God's strength and resources.

Today, I declare over you — you are an overcomer, marching toward your destiny in God.

Today, I declare in His name, that you will have the outlook of a champion. Champions don't hesitate to get back in the ring. You have already won! You know you will win again.

We must look FROM victory – not TO victory!

Champions aren't afraid of the enemy and his lies; they know the Lord has crushed them. Losing is never an option. In fact, Jeremiah 20:11 tells us "The Lord is with me like a mighty warrior; so my persecutors will stumble and not prevail. They will fail and be thoroughly disgraced; their dishonor will never be forgotten."

You and I won when Jesus died and rose again. He defeated death so that we can reign victorious in this life. We must not talk ourselves out of the victory that we already have.

Today, you are a Champion! Now is the time to live like it!

First John 5:4 *"For everyone born of God overcomes the world. This is the victory that has overcome the world, even our faith."*

When we allow God's Spirit to lead us, we produce good things: *"But the fruit of the Spirit is love, joy, peace, longsuffering, gentleness, goodness, faith, meekness, temperance: against such there is no law"* (Galatians 5:22, 23).

As we abide in Christ Jesus, we are changed and become more like Him! Soon we will be living and acting in ways that reflect His living on the inside of us. We will be showing outwardly the blessings that we received inwardly.

Today, allow yourself to walk after the Spirit. Keep yourself attuned to God's voice, make choices in line with God's Word and show the fruit of the Spirit as you go about your day.

PRAYER POINT

Lord, I pray that I will clearly hear, "You are a Champion." Help me to realize that I am a Champion in Christ and give me certainty that I was created for this high purpose. May the eyes of my understanding be enlightened so that I will know what is the hope of Your calling (Ephesians 1:18). Lord, when You call us, You also enable us, and I know that you have enabled me to be a Champion. Enable me to walk worthy of my calling and become the Champion You made me to be.

Continue to remind me that I am a Champion in Christ and don't let me get sidetracked. Strike down discouragement so that it will not defeat me. Lift my eyes above the circumstances of the moment so I can see the purpose for which You created me. Give me patience to wait for Your perfect timing. I pray that the desires of my heart will not be in conflict with the desires of Your heart. May I seek You for direction and hear when You speak to me! Amen.

> If Captain Crunch Berries aren't considered fresh fruit I don't think this diet is going to work out

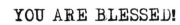

YOU ARE BLESSED!

The word "blessed" means happy, fortunate, prosperous, and enviable. Roll the words around and around in your heart and mind and let the Lord speak to you about them.

(Psalm 1:1-3)

Blessed is the one
who does not walk in step with the wicked
or stand in the way that sinners take
or sit in the company of mockers,
but whose delight is in the law of the Lord,
and who meditates on His law day and night.
That person is like a tree planted by streams of
water, which yields its fruit in season
and whose leaf does not wither –
whatever they do prospers.

Blessing Confessions

Today, I want to begin by counting some of my many blessings! Would you join me? Meditating on God's Word is vital to our spiritual growth. It doesn't matter if you are an old-timer, a babe in Christ, or a believer who is facing spiritual warfare. Confessing what is rightfully yours in Christ can be a powerful spiritual tool to build up your faith, encourage you spiritually and help make you more available to receive all the good things that God has made available to you! It is by knowing God's love that we are able to experience the fullness of God in our lives.

Ephesians 3:19 says, *"and to know this love that surpasses knowledge... that you may be filled to the measure of all the fullness of God."*

There's something about a verbal confession that makes things sink in much deeper. In meditating on the good things that God has done for us, we realize the great love that God has for us. I encourage you to speak each blessing listed below out loud to yourself:

- I am blessed because I was uniquely handmade by the King of Kings: Psalm 139:14, *"I praise you because I am fearfully and wonderfully made; your works are wonderful, I know that full well."*
- I am loved so much that God sent His Son to die as a symbol of His great love for me: 1 John 4:9, *"This is how God showed His love among us: He sent His one and only Son into the world that we might live through Him."*
- I am loved so much, that a big party was thrown in heaven when I was adopted into the royal family: Luke 15:10, *"In the same way, I tell you, there is rejoicing in the presence of the angels of God over one sinner who repents."*
- My past has been washed away, and I have been given a completely new identity through Christ: 2 Corinthians 5:17 *"Therefore, if anyone is in Christ, the new creation has come: The old has gone, the new is here!"*
- My heavenly Father loves me so much that He wanted me to be His child: 1 John 3:1, *"See what great love the Father has lavished on us, that we should be called children of God."*
- I am blessed because there is no condemnation awaiting me: Romans 8:1, *"Therefore, there is now no condemnation for those who are in Christ Jesus."*
- I am blessed because my sins are not only forgiven, but God Himself chose to forget them: Isaiah 43:25, *"I, even I, am He who blots out your transgressions, for My own sake, and remembers your sins no more."*

- I am blessed because God thinks wonderful things towards me: Psalm 139:17, *"How precious to me are Your thoughts, God! How vast is the sum of them!"*

- I am entitled to complete physical healing and deliverance from evil spirits through the work Christ did on the cross for me: Isaiah 53:5, *"But He was pierced for our transgressions, He was crushed for our iniquities, the punishment that brought us peace was on Him, and by His wounds we are healed."* And Matthew 8:16-17, *"When evening came, many who were demon-possessed were brought to Him, and He drove out the spirits with a word and healed all the sick. This was to fulfill what was spoken through the prophet Isaiah: "He took up our infirmities and bore our diseases.'"*

- I was not given a spirit of fear, but of love and a sound mind: 2 Timothy 1:7, *"For the Spirit God gave us does not make us timid, but gives us power, love and self-discipline."* Romans 8:15, *"The Spirit you received does not make you slaves, so that you live in fear again; rather, the Spirit you received brought about your adoption to sonship. And by Him we cry, "Abba, Father."*

- My heavenly Father loves to bring me joy by answering my prayers: John 16:24, *"Until now you have not asked for anything in My name. Ask and you will receive, and your joy will be complete."*

- I have a future awaiting me that is beyond what the human mind can comprehend: 1 Corinthians 2:9, *"However, as it is written: "What no eye has seen, what no ear has heard, and what no human mind has conceived"* – *the things God has prepared for those who love Him –* "

All I can say is, "Thank you Jesus!!!!!"

PRAYER POINT

Thank You Lord that I have the mind of Christ (Philippians 2:5). I have chosen to live by Your Spirit of Wisdom. My mind is focused on You, Lord, and the truth of Your Word. My ear is tuned to hear Your words of counsel. I seek Your instruction which is true, vibrant and life-giving. I have chosen to have You direct my life: You alone, Lord, and no one else. Nothing else.

You have caused me, Lord, to be like a tree planted and tended beside a sure river. You are the River, Lord. My roots go deep down into You. So I am confident that if there is drought all around me, I will not wilt. I will not faint. You sustain me, Lord through economic crisis. And, I say, *"Taste and see that the Lord is good"* (Psalm 34:8).

I draw on Your living water today, Lord, to nourish and refresh the spiritual fruit developing in my life. Thank You for Your water that never runs dry.

And thank You for the prospering You cause in my life. I prosper now in my spirit, my soul, and my body. O God, I am blessed. Alleluia! Amen!

> Going to the dentist this morning and it hit me — if a dentist makes money off people with unhealthy teeth, why should we trust a toothbrush that 4 out of 5 dentists recommend?

Living In His Authority

INTRODUCTION

It's Monday! So, you're walking along, going about your daily routine, and minding your business, when... BAM!! Out of nowhere, someone, something, somehow, you find yourself in the middle of a full on attack of the enemy.

He's coming full-throttle, hitting all of your buttons, tapping all of your soft spots, and taking you to that place that brings out the worst in you, all in one fell swoop. Before you can think, you're reacting, striking back with what you've got, but not thinking about who you are, who you represent, and who just might be watching you.

Then it's over. You're left wondering how in the world you got so far out of line. You marvel at the way you behaved and feel the twinge of guilt recognizing that you slipped so badly.

Sneak attacks from the enemy are the worst. This is why the Bible tells us to be vigilant and always on guard against him.

First Peter 5:8 *"Be alert and of sober mind. Your enemy the devil prowls around like a roaring lion looking for someone to devour."* The devil is always searching for an opening; it's our job not to give him any room. Keep your guard up by meditating on God's Word and keeping in constant communication with the Holy Spirit.

Feed yourself on His Word, so that it will be the river of life that flows out of you no matter what comes your way. As you keep your ears inclined to God's Word and daily directed by the Holy Spirit, He will guide you in all truths. No matter what crosses your path, you can be assured that

Introduction

your response will originate out of the love of God and the power of the Holy Spirit.

Never fall victim to the sneak attack again!

First Peter 5:9 goes on to say, *"Resist him, standing firm in the faith, because you know that the family of believers throughout the world is undergoing the same kind of sufferings."*

Today, we are going to resist the devil through an exercise of our faith. We are going to call things that are not as though they were (Romans 4:17). We are going to speak life over our day, and watch the Lord put His power behind our words:

- Today will be a great day in Jesus name! Today will be a day filled with unexpected blessings, opportunities to share my faith, and moments to spend time with God!
- I will not be overwhelmed or stressed out today! I will be able to meet every challenge and solve every problem. The Holy Spirit dwells inside of me, and He helps me in every situation!

"No weapon formed against us shall prosper, and every tongue that rises up against us shall fall. This is the heritage of the servants of the LORD" (Isaiah 54:17).

Listen, Jesus had all authority:
- Authority to command the wind and waves
- Authority to heal the crippled
- Authority to open blinded eyes
- Authority to resurrect the dead.
- Authority to cast out devils

AND, Jesus gave authority to you and to me: Matthew 10:1, *"And when He had called unto Him His twelve disciples, He gave them power against unclean spirits, to cast them out, and to heal all manner of sickness and all manner of disease."*

Hallelujah!

Now let's get to it. So standing in the authority I have as a Spirit-Filled follower of Jesus Christ, I proclaim for myself and my family and friends:

- Divine healing and divine health!
- Deliverance and freedom!
- Full restoration, double restoration, and seven restorations!
- Inner healing and sound mental health!
- Grace and mercy!
- Rest and peace for me!
- The renewing of the minds!
- Personal God encounters
- The Presence and fullness of the Holy Spirit!

At the end of the day, we will be smiling because of what the Lord was able to do through us.

> We had a power outage last week and my PC, TV and games console shut down immediately, so I had to talk to my family for a few hours. They seem like nice people.

OUR AUTHORITY IN PRAYER

Let's talk about prayer and our authority as Christians. In Exodus 14:15-16, we read: *"Then the LORD said to Moses, 'Why are you crying out to Me? Tell the Israelites to move on. Raise your staff and stretch out your hand over the sea to divide the water so that the Israelites can go through the sea on dry ground.'"*

The problem with many of us in the body of Christ today is not that we are not praying. We are praying, but many of us are praying desperate prayers. We are praying, "God, help… God, please… God, do something about my problem!"

If you are smiling a little by now, you know about such prayers and might even have prayed a couple yourself. I know I have.

God does not want you to pray pleading prayers all the time. He wants you to use the authority He has given you to pray powerful prayers, to boldly command and to "stretch out your hand" and see miracles happen.

When Moses stood before the Red Sea with Pharaoh's army in hot pursuit, the Bible tells us that he cried out to God. But God told him, "Why do you cry to Me?" There is a time for you to cry out to God and there is a time for you to use your authority. God told Moses, "Tell the children of Israel to go forward. But lift up your rod, and stretch out your hand over the sea and divide it."

The "rod" you have today is the name of Jesus. As you command in Jesus' name, your "sea" will open and you will walk on dry ground through the midst of your problem.

Do you realize that Jesus did not say, "Go and pray for the sick?" He said, "Go and heal the sick." (Matthew 10:8) So stop pleading and asking all the time, and start using the authority you have in Christ.

Jesus told the church, *"All authority has been given to Me in heaven and on earth. Go therefore..."* (Matthew 28:18-19) God wants you to go and use the authority that He has given you. And as you go, miracles will flow!

When you start using the authority you have in Christ, you will experience miracles! Let's give it a try right now.

PRAYER POINT

In the Name of Jesus Christ, by the Power of His Blood and in the authority of His Word given to me as a Christian: I bind and reject you satan and I command you to leave. I seal this home and place of my employment, and all the members of my family, friends, relatives and possessions, in the Blood of the Lord Jesus Christ.

I bind and reject all spirits of confusion, disruption, division, fear, disbelief, deaf and dumb, and disobedience, and the spirit of games. I break and dissolve every curse, spell, evil word spoken over me. I ask this in the name of Jesus Christ, by the power of His blood, and in the authority of His Word given to me as a Christian. Amen.

> Just like our bodies, our minds need exercise. That's why I think of jogging every morning.

BENEFITS OF EMPOWERMENT

Call it fire, zeal or passion. Whatever the term, it is the strong feeling you have for God and your faith. At one time or another in your life, you can go through a season when you feel you have lost this enthusiasm or feel abandoned by Him when circumstances in your life seem overwhelming. In order to rekindle a passion for God, you must be open and honest in your communication and relationship with God.

The truth is that it's a new day and you and I are children of the King! As a child of the King, you now have an incredible inheritance, a big part of which is available in this life. At birth, God gives each of us natural gifts such as artistic, musical, athletic or intellectual ability. After you become a believer, the Holy Spirit also gave you supernatural, miracle-working gifts (I Corinthians 12).

When you were "born-again," you were given the authority of a son or daughter of the King, the Most High God. The Bible says ALL authority was given to Jesus (Matthew 28:18). Jesus Himself then said He gave supernatural authority to His followers (Luke 10:19) so they might do the works He did (John 14: 11-12).

TODAY YOU HAVE BEEN EMPOWERED!

And there are benefits of this Holy Spirit empowerment:

- Passion for God – You will have an increased hunger for God and all the things of God. You will move into deeper levels of prayer and worship. You will better understand God's nature, personality, power and Word.

- Passion of God – You will become more concerned about the things God is most concerned about. God will give you His concern for the lost. He will even give you love and compassion for people you don't even know. You will have a new compassion for the hurting and wounded.

- Power of God – You will immediately begin to experience God's supernatural power in your life. Large and small miracles will begin to occur in your life, and in the lives of those you pray for, as you walk in the power of the Holy Spirit.

- Sensitivity to God – You will develop a higher level of receptivity to the leading of the Holy Spirit and become much more aware of God's divine intervention and angelic activity around you. You will talk to God and will actually hear Him communicate back to you in a variety of creative ways.

Where does this kind of passion for God come from? It comes from an understanding of who He is and who we are. It comes with the realization of what He has done for us, and the reality of His overwhelming passionate love for you!

PRAYER POINT

Below is a prayer guide to get you started. I wonder what God might do if these 12 requests rose to the top of our personal prayers.

- Pray for a growing personal passion for God and His Word.
- Pray for a growing hunger and thirst for righteousness.
- Pray for solid spiritual growth and fruit.
- Pray for growing love and care for others.
- Pray for revival in your church.
- Pray for a growing passion for evangelism and missions.
- Pray for personal opportunities for evangelism.
- Pray for a willingness to go and for boldness and wisdom in sharing the gospel.
- Pray for a great spiritual awakening in your life, in the lives of your family members and in your church.
- Pray for your life and your family's lives to be strengthened with power to persevere with joy.
- Pray for strength, safety, health, and opportunities to spread the gospel with your friends.
- Pray for a greater personal spiritual awakening.

COURAGE TAKES ACTION!

Step Out! Make a Move!

It is one thing to believe God will bring you to your Promised Land and it is another to never step one foot towards that promise. We cannot expect to advance and take the land if we stay in one place. God is waiting for you to step out.

The fear of stepping in the wrong direction is bondage. If you never step, you will never obtain. I believe if you step in the wrong direction, God will lovingly correct you if your heart is to do His will and to please Him.

Stand in the confidence of whose you are.

Step out in faith and believe God will move after you move, just like the priests who had to step into the water with the Ark of the Covenant. Once they took a step, the waters began to part. Before they took the step, the waters never moved (Joshua 3).

I like what Hebrews 10:35-39 says, *"So do not throw away your confidence; it will be richly rewarded. You need to persevere so that when you have done the will of God, you will receive what He has promised. For, 'In just a little while, He who is coming will come and will not delay.' And, 'But my righteous one will live by faith. And I take no pleasure in the one who shrinks back.' But we do not belong to those who shrink back and are destroyed, but to those who have faith and are saved."*

Retreating is the opposite of taking a step forward towards your fears. What does a step forward look like? It can come in the form of tearing down imaginations that try to become greater than the knowledge of God in your heart (2 Corinthians 10:5). It is bringing every thought into captivity to the obedience of Christ.

Another form of stepping towards your fears can be doing the exact opposite of what your flesh tells you. If you are afraid of men and what they think of you, then

Courage Takes Action

you need to function and walk where you think people are having a problem with you and love them unconditionally. How about facing the very person that hurt you in your past and forgive them?

One of the biggest things we can do is to confront the enemy and cast him down. We have let him have a stronghold for too long and it's time for us to take our authority and command him to leave us. Courage is a wonderful character trait if we let it be complete in us. Courage is nothing if we don't act upon it.

PRAYER POINT

Lord, may Your Holy Spirit empower me to take action where You have called me to move. May I not be swayed by the fear of people, but may I hold firm to the power of the Holy Spirit.

Lord, put courage into my heart and take away all that may hinder me serving You. Holy Spirit, empower my tongue to proclaim your goodness, so that all may understand me. Give me courageous Christian friends to advise and help me, so that by working together our efforts may bear abundant fruit. Above all, let me constantly remember that all of my actions are in vain unless they are guided by your hand.

Shout-out to God for not giving wings to snakes.

FEAR NOT!

Fear can be complex and all-encompassing thing: Fear of the unknown. Fear of the known. Fear of success. Fear of failure. Fear of rejection. Fear of living up to expectations.

Many people's whole lives are dictated by their fears. They get so caught up in what might happen that they react in ways that actually impede their progress.

That's the crazy thing about fear. We don't know for certain what's coming next. Fear presents such a convincing case that we fall victim to its piercing words. We may not know for a fact, but the possibility is so scary, that we adjust our behavior accordingly.

The Bible states that God hasn't given us a spirit of fear (2 Timothy 1:7). In fact, we are empowered, calmed, and loved through the Holy Spirit that God has filled us with. However, we often choose to embrace fear.

We get caught up in our thoughts or in our perception of what others are thinking about us. We forget about the Greater One who resides on the inside of us and all the promises He has given us. We believe the mirage which fear so readily paints in our field of vision.

Don't let fear keep you from your purpose in God. Remember that you have been blessed with power, love and a sound mind. There is nothing fear can produce that can overcome your Heavenly Father's will for your life. As long as you stand firmly planted, believing what God has to say, Fear can never have its way with you again.

Psalm 27:1 *"The LORD is my light and my salvation – whom shall I fear? The LORD is the stronghold of my life – of whom shall I be afraid?"*

Jesus understands that fear is a strong emotion. Because of that dark night in Gethsemane, He knows firsthand what fear is like. In spite of that, He can still tell us, "Don't be afraid."

In our attempt to obey that command, willpower alone just doesn't cut it. We can try to squelch our fearful thoughts, but they just keep popping up, like a ball held under water.

To take authority in this area, two things are necessary. First, we have to acknowledge that fear is too strong for us, so only God can handle it. We have to turn our fears over to Him, remembering that He is all-powerful, all-knowing, and always in control.

Second, we have to replace a bad habit of having "fear thoughts" with a good habit: namely prayer and confidence in the working of the Holy Spirit. We may be able to switch thoughts with lightning speed, but we can't think about two things at once. Therefore, if we're praying and thanking God for His help, we can't be thinking about fear at the same time.

Fear does not have to be a lifelong battle, but God is our lifelong Protector. He promised to never abandon or forsake us. When we are secure in His love and salvation and the working of the Holy Spirit, nothing can snatch us from Him, not even death. By holding tightly to God, no matter what, we will make it through as the victors we are and not be filled with fear.

PRAYER POINT

I declare that greater is the One who is in me than any devil on the side of my enemy.

You, spirit of fear, are not on God's agenda for me. I dismiss you from my life now, in the name of Jesus. Jesus said that even the very hairs of my head are not only counted but numbered. Not one single strand can be removed without God's knowledge and permission. Knowing that I have a God who cares about every little detail of my life, I put my confidence in the Lord.

In the name of Jesus, I break the power of fear, because God has not given me the spirit of fear, but of power and of love and of a sound mind. I bind the spirit of fear in my life, in the name of Jesus. I break every evil covenant that has brought fear into my life, in the name of Jesus. Spirit of fear, you must loose your hold upon my life and my family, in the name of Jesus. My tomorrow is blessed in Christ Jesus; therefore, in Jesus name, I bind the spirit that is responsible for the fear of tomorrow.

I receive and embrace the power, love and sound mind that God has given me through His Holy Spirit. Amen.

> These are **not pizza** stains **on my shirt**; they are **pizza memories, wonderful, wonderful memories.**

ARE YOU FREE... ENOUGH?

Here is a question for all of us to ask: "Am I free enough in myself to do whatever He asks?" Wow! Not an easy one to answer in all honesty.

To obey the voice of God means more than "committing the matter to prayer!" The voice of God demands an action on our part—a demonstration that we believe what He says is true. Once we learn that kind of obedience, we discover the Holy Spirit opening doors of opportunity to us, and providing our every need to fulfill those opportunities!

Recently, the Holy Spirit spoke to me these words: "Right now many of My people are hearing My voice, but they are not free enough in themselves to obey Me." It is important for us to learn that with the voice of God speaking to us today, He is giving us the "keys" to fulfill our destiny in a supernatural way.

There is a solution to this problem of being free found in these Scriptures:

Galatians 5:16-18 *"So I say, walk by the Spirit, and you will not gratify the desires of the flesh. For the flesh desires what is contrary to the Spirit, and the Spirit what is contrary to the flesh. They are in conflict with each other, so that you are not to do whatever you want. But if you are led by the Spirit, you are not under the law."*

Romans 8:1-6 *"Therefore, there is now no condemnation for those who are in Christ Jesus, because through Christ Jesus the law of the Spirit who gives life has set you free from the law of sin and death. For what the law was powerless to do because it was weakened by the flesh, God did by sending his own Son in the likeness of sinful flesh to be a sin offering. And so he condemned sin in the flesh, in order that the righteous requirement of the law might be fully met in us, who do not live according to the flesh but according to the Spirit. Those who live according to the flesh have their minds set on what the flesh desires; but those who live in accordance with the Spirit have their minds set on what the Spirit desires. The mind governed by the flesh is death, but the mind governed by the Spirit is life and peace."*

The solution to being "free enough" is to live in the Spirit: filling your life with the things of the Spirit and directing your mind onto the desires of the Spirit so that "the flesh" and its interests do not get a hook into your life. Regularly talk to the Father and enjoy the Presence and leading of the Holy Spirit. Read your Bible with fresh eyes and Holy Spirit interaction. Each day, proclaim over yourself that you are a "King's Kid" and that you are living in freedom, victory and destiny. Develop honest relationships with other believers. The more time you spend in the Holy Spirit, the less time there will be for self-defeat.

Proclaim these over your life:

- Grace – for God to be kind toward you and give you many undeserved favors along with the power to overcome and live free!
- Mercy - for God to deliver you from the messes you get yourself into, especially when you are ignorant or foolish.
- Peace – allow His peace to be the umpire over conflicts and guide you in your decisions.
- Understanding – for God's perspective as to the heart of the matter.
- Wisdom & Discernment - so you can apply His understanding to your real-life situations.
- Filled With The Love of God – being saturated with His love makes thinking His thoughts easy.
- Filled With The Spirit – one with His Spirit in heart and mind; overflowing with joy.

I am free, not because I am perfect or "getting it right." It is because I am covered by Jesus who is Righteousness. I am safe in Him, alive in Him, forgiven and set free. I am saved by Jesus!

PRAYER POINT

Oh, Jesus! THANK YOU! Thank You for loving me. Thank You for opening my heart to receive You. Thank You for living in me. You are the Living Word. Come deeper! Cut out everything not of You. Refine me. Wash my feet daily. Help me to confess everything so that nothing is hiding from You.

You are so wonderful, Lord. Let my life bring You praise. Make us One! Let your Spirit flow through me and fill me and overtake me! I am Yours, now and forever. Nothing can snatch me from Your hands. I am not afraid. What can man do to me? Even if I die, I live.

Speak, Lord. I am listening. Let me feast on You, the Bread of Life. Quench my thirst with Your Living Water. Let me only be satisfied by You. I want to see You, to know You more. Come, Lord Jesus! Live in every cell of my body. Let Your blood flow through my veins. Transform me. Let Your Truth be the light that guides me. Illuminate my path. You are the Way. Lead me on level paths for Your Name's Sake.

By the power of Your Spirit in us, let Your body—the church—speak in a language that all can hear and understand. Restore all things. Reconcile all to you! Bring your freedom. Break every chain. Remove every obstacle. In the name of Jesus, Amen.

PRAYER FOR FINANCES

This prayer and confession will help you to release your faith and exercise your authority over your own finances and the enemy's schemes. We must stand our ground and believe God. I encourage you to frequently read this out loud.

Part of the power of this prayer is in recognizing and confessing that the problem is too big for you but is manageable by God. This is an important big step. You roll the burden of the problem onto the Burden Bearer, just as Jesus instructed. (Matthew 11:30)

As you pray, instead of allowing fear to grip you, your mind will be renewed. You will begin to see your financial situation from God's perspective. This increases faith tremendously and when you have faith the size of a mustard seed, *"you will say to this mountain, 'move from here to there,' and it will move; and nothing will be impossible for you"* (Matthew 17:20).

How to pray this Prayer and confession:

- Pray it each day, taking authority over the thief for this day.
- Any time during the day. When your financial situation comes to mind, pray the prayer again.
- Pray this instead of worrying.

I am standing with you **IN THE AUTHORITY OF A BELIEVER!**

The following is your Confession to Take Authority over Your Finances:

PRAYER POINT

Lord, I come to You today in the name of Your Son, Jesus. You said in John 16:23-24, *"In that day you will no longer ask Me anything. Very truly I tell you, My Father will give you whatever you ask in My Name. Until now you have not asked for anything in My Name. Ask and you will receive, and your joy will be complete."*

I am asking for a miracle in my finances: something that I can't do, but is entirely possible for You. In Mark 10:27, You said, *"With man this is impossible, but not with God; all things are possible with God."*

Lord, You are the only One who can turn this financial situation around for my good and in my favor. So, I am asking You for my all of my accounts to be paid in full. By faith, I receive my miracle now and I thank You that You've granted me favor.

Enemy, I take authority over you in the Name of Jesus. You will not keep me from receiving my miracle, for is written, *"Greater is He that is in me than he that is in the world."*

It is also written that whatever I bind on earth is bound in heaven. Satan, I bind you from everything that concerns my financial matters, in Jesus' Name. You will not keep me from paying any of my bills; you'll not keep any money from coming to me.

I refuse debt, lack, and poverty, for my God supplies all of my need, according to His riches in glory by Christ Jesus.

I only accept abundance, and I refuse to live in poverty and lack, for is written that I am an heir of God, a joint-heir with Christ Jesus, and an heir of Abraham's blessings. Financial blessings can't be stopped from coming to me, for Jesus gave me power to tread on serpents and scorpions, and over all the power the enemy (Luke 10:19).

Enemy, you can't keep me from having favor with God and man, for I have authority over you, in Jesus' Name.

Father, I'm Your child and I'm a tither. You promised me in Your Word that You would open up the windows of heaven and pour me out a blessing, and that You would rebuke the devourer for my sake.

Jesus came that I might have life and have it more abundantly. You promised that everything I would do would prosper. You promised I would lack no good thing, and that You would withhold no good thing from me. You promised that You would never leave me nor forsake me, and I believe that You are with me in this financial matter.

Lord, I know there is nothing too difficult for You to do. Father, I thank You that the devil is bound from my finances and that he cannot keep any money or any favor from coming to me. I am expecting my financial miracle, for Your Name's Sake. Amen.

WINNERS AND CHAMPIONS

Here is a thought for today: We can choose to just be a winner, or we can upgrade to Champion status.

As Christians, our faith in God has automatically granted us the name of Winner through Christ's death and resurrection. We don't have to fear death because we know that we will live eternally with Christ. In fact, we need not fear at all as we are Kingdom people and over-comers RIGHT NOW! However, a lot of us miss out on the chance to be victorious in every situation, not just our spiritual redemption.

A Champion is one who has overcome every opponent. They are undefeated. Every challenge they have faced, they have won. Every winner can't say that they're a Champion.

As believers, God has promised us that we can be Champions too! First John 5:4 states: *"For everyone born of God overcomes the world. This is the victory that has overcome the world, even our faith."* If you have been born of God, you can overcome the world!

Yet so many times, we let situations and circumstances tell us that we are going to lose.

We believe the lie of the enemy and give up the fight; or even worse, we do not fight at all. We settle to just be winners over those things that we believe we can do, when we can be Champions over it all.

Don't let the world talk you out of your victory. Ignore the circumstances that tell you that you don't have the strength, the money, the connections, the health...whatever it is that they say you need. You have everything you need in Christ Jesus!

"Greater is He that is in you than he that is in the world" (1 John 4:4), and the "He" that is in you has told you that you can overcome the world!

So, don't choose to lose! Stand in the victory that is already yours, you mighty CHAMPION! Keep pressing. Keep believing. Keep your faith strong. YOU WIN! You are a CHAMPION!

First Corinthians 15:57, *"But thanks be to God! He gives us the victory through our Lord Jesus Christ."*

Here is a special breakdown of the word "Champion" to help you in your prayers today.

C.H.A.M.P.I.O.N. stands for:

Christ has eliminated my guilt

His Spirit tells me I am His child

Awesome victory is mine

My mind is set on His Spirit

Power is made perfect in weakness

I have the intercession of the Holy Spirit and Jesus

Only God knows why bad things happen to good people

Nothing separates me from His love

SATAN HAS BEEN DEFEATED!!!

PRAYER POINT

Dear Lord, today I ask that You help me live to the level of greatness You have already placed in me. I do know that I am already a victor in Your eyes. Jesus, release me from all worries, fears and doubts so that I may concentrate on KINGDOM truths. Make me fearless. In You, we are all victorious.

Jesus, I thank You that You have made all Your children forever champions and winners. Amen.

> That moment when you pour yourself a bowl of cereal and discover there's no milk. So you just sit there, wondering why bad things happen to good people.

YOU WANT TO GO DEEPER?

Have you ever noticed that sometimes church people like to sound spiritual by saying, "I want to go deeper." To me, this is one of the most overused and often overrated comment people make in church. I say this because it often reflects a person's desire to be thought of as pious or spiritual.

So rather than throw this statement out, I want to reclaim and redefine it. What does "go deeper" mean to me? It means three things:

1. <u>Going Deeper into My Commitment to God's Church.</u>
   I can't be committed to Jesus (the head) without being committed to the church (His body). I must love God's people with the same fervor and passion that I have for Him. I can't say I love and serve Jesus if I don't also love and serve His Bride.

2. <u>Going Deeper into My Commitment to the World</u>.
   The world is dying and lost without Jesus. If I am to "go deeper," I must dive deeper into the muck and mire of a broken world in order to reach people. God is assembling an army of believers who are willing to pursue their spiritual and natural inheritance right now (Matthew 25:34). This army is not waiting to make a quick escape to Heaven; they are changing cities and nations now. They even believe they are commissioned to "disciple nations" and that it is possible to change this world instead of abandoning it. Amazing!

3. <u>Going Deeper into My Commitment to Living as a Child of the King!</u>
   Because of who Jesus Christ is, and because He is my Savior and my Lord:

   - I am a child of the King of Kings and Lord of Lords, seated with Christ in the heavenly realm. I am chosen, accepted, and included — a citizen of heaven and a member of God's household.
   - I am loved by God unconditionally and without reservation.
   - I am a Christian. I am not just different in what I do. My identity has changed. Who I am has changed. Everything has become brand new.
   - I am a dwelling place in which God lives by His Spirit. I have access to Him anytime, anywhere, for any reason.
   - I am God's creation – His workmanship. I was created by Him and for Him, so who I am and what I do matters. I am spiritually alive. I have been set free from the fear of death and have been given life to live and enjoy to the full.
   - I am forgiven – completely, totally, and absolutely.
   - If God is for me, it doesn't matter who or what stands against me, because nothing and no one can separate me from the love of Christ — not hurt, pain, loss, problem, or brokenness; not persecution, trouble, difficulty, or danger; not abandonment, abuse, addictions, or appetites; not desires, food, sexuality, or relationships; not life or death, angels or demons; not my past, the present, or the future; no power, no person, no place, not anything in all creation; not even Satan himself shall prevail.

- I Am a Child of the King and choose this day to live as one.
- I belong to Him, having been bought by Him with the precious blood of Jesus. I have eternal life and will be saved from all of God's wrath to come—guaranteed!

If you want to go Deeper, come out of hiding

God knows everything about you and loves you anyway. Decide to stop trying to control your life and withholding your trust from God. Commit every part of your life to Him so you can experience positive transformation and freedom.

You want to go deeper? Focus on who you are rather than what you do. The many roles you fill in life (as a spouse, parent, friend, employee, volunteer, etc.), while important, don't represent who you are as a person. Instead of basing your identity on roles that can change, base it on God's love for you, which will never change. Place your confidence in who you are (someone created by God) and whose you are (someone who belongs to God).

You want to go deeper? Immerse yourself in Scripture. Every day, make time to read, study, and meditate on some passages from the Bible. Absorb Scripture deep into your soul, where its truths will transform you. When you make decisions, look to biblical principles rather than just your own feelings for guidance.

You want to go deeper? Trust God. Every fear you hold onto blocks you from experiencing a deeper relationship with God, because it undermines the trust on which a close relationship is based.

PRAYER POINT

Lord, I come to You with a willingness to enter the deeper places of the Spirit. Draw me, Lord, where I might experience all that is on Your heart. I want to know You in a new and a fresh way, and I lay down my own time and agenda today that I may go deeper in You!

In Jesus' Name, Amen!

**BOTTOM LINE -- A real friend is someone who knows how totally crazy you are...
But is still willing to be seen out in public with you.**

Living a Hope-Filled Life

INTRODUCTION

Even when life is tough you can be filled with hope. You will find that hope will strengthen you mentally, emotionally and spiritually to hold onto your faith in God's promises until you see their fulfillment.

With the grace of God to enable you, you will discover God working more powerfully when you are the weakest, you have no strength, and you have no reason to believe things are going to change. This is the time for the hope of God to work most effectively. Just throw yourself on the mercy and the grace of God that has never failed anyone.

Our hope begins and ends with God. We believe that there is no true, lasting hope in this world without God. He is the God who made us: the personal God, who loves us and who wants to give meaning and purpose to each of our lives.

The Lord withholds no good thing—including His favor when you need His help. If you have tried to make it without God, you probably know how frustrating it can be. Without God's power, we have no hope of overcoming our struggles. Without God's mercy, we have no hope of overcoming our past. Without the meaning that God gives to life, or the sense of purpose that He provides, we have no hope of overcoming the problems that life presents.

God's revealed Word—the Bible—tells us that God has continually called people to be in a relationship with Him. He is not an indifferent God, but One who desires to interact with His creation—you and me! Through His Word, God gives us instruction and understanding about how to live in relationship with Him, with one another and

Introduction

have a life with vision and purpose. These are not arbitrary rules and regulations, but things that actually work for our good.

Personal belief in God and trusting in His promises fill our lives with hope. God wants to be in a relationship with us. He wants us to talk with Him every day. He wants to provide what we need for this life and provide us with a life that has no end. What better hope could there be than that?

We believe there is hope for life. It is our conviction that you can have a life of hope, joy, peace, purpose and glory. That hope is found in God. He made you, loves you, and wants the best for you—both now and forever. To make sure you found your way to Him, God did an extraordinary thing: He sent his Son Jesus to show you the way. Jesus Himself said, *"I am the way, the truth, and the life"* (John 14:6). The living way to God is found in His Son, Christ Jesus.

Hebrews 4:16 *"Let us then approach God's throne of grace with confidence, so that we may receive mercy and find grace to help us in our time of need."*

Going to the throne room to receive His grace, His favor, and His help is precisely what the Lord God wants you to do. Even in your failures, He wants you to run to the Throne Room and find His strength, wisdom and power to help you. The Lord of mercy and grace sits on His throne, waiting for you to come and receive His help. It will be appropriate, well-timed help, coming just when you need it.

Where there is God, there is hope.

What about you? Will you choose to acknowledge God's presence and awareness of your situation? Will you put your hope in Him to accomplish what's best? If so, your hopelessness will give way to hope for each day.

That's not all. Joy is also a great antidote for hopelessness. Romans 15:13 is my wife's favorite scripture: *"May the God of hope fill you with all joy and peace as you trust in Him, so that you may overflow with hope by the power of the Holy Spirit."*

May the hope that's found in Christ alone be yours today.

> Truth is--I prefer not to think before I speak. I like being just as surprised as everyone else by what comes out of my mouth.

HE WILL DO WHAT IS BEST... FOR YOU

Life is filled with numerous uncertainties. We do not always know what will happen in our lives. Though this is true, believers should not walk around in doubt and fear. Once we have received Christ, we can trust that He will be with us at all times.

There is never a time when He is not present. He is there; He cares and offers help. Today, remind yourself of His presence in your life. The enemy would like you to doubt God and His assurance when He said that He would never leave us nor forsake us.

Hebrews 13:5 *"God has said, 'Never will I leave you; never will I forsake you.'"*

So if you are wondering how the situation is going to turn out, stop and know that He will do what is best for you. If you are wondering if He is going to answer that prayer, stop and know that His ears are open to the cries of His people. If you are wondering if He sees and knows what you are going through, stop and know that His eyes are upon the righteous.

Just in case you are wondering if He is there or if He cares or if He will forgive, remember that He is God and He does not change. Do not think you can make God change His mind concerning you, because His thoughts toward you are for good and He will bring forth good in every situation.

PRAYER POINT

Lord, I pray that You would give me a confident heart in Christ. Take me beyond believing in You to truly believing You. Help me rely on the power of Your promises and live like they are true. You say blessed is the one who trusts in You and whose hope and confidence are found in You. Those who hope in You will not be disappointed, because You work all things together for good for those who love You and are called according to Your purpose.

When self-doubt tells me I can't overcome my insecurities, I will believe Your promise that all things are possible to whoever believes. I will not throw away my confidence, because You say it will be richly rewarded. I will persevere so that when I have done the will of God, I will receive what You have promised. My confidence is in Christ and I am no longer one who shrinks back and is destroyed, but one who believes and is saved!

In Jesus' name, Amen.

> Ladies, any perfume that claims it will help you catch the attention of your man is lying...
> unless it smells like pizza

WHEN YOU FEEL LOST

Feeling lost?

Sometimes in life we lose our way and wake up one day wondering how we got to where we are. The place we find ourselves seems foreign. We know we are not walking in all of the blessings Father God has for us, but we don't know how to get back to Him.

Sometimes life is full of challenges, and it can even seem hopeless at times. Life can often be confusing and sometimes we feel an ache inside that we don't understand. These things can cause us to feel depressed and lonely, and our thoughts can go in crazy directions. But I want you to know this; we have all gone through some of what you might be feeling right now. It seems like our emotions begin to take over and we feel alienated from God and our family and friends. We don't know how to explain what's wrong because we don't always understand it ourselves. It would be great if everything was just perfect all of the time and we wouldn't have these empty and useless feelings inside.

Here are some things to remember when you go through these difficulties. Know this first, in those times when we feel lost and alone, God is still there reaching out to us. God is right by our side when we are afraid of what we are facing, unsure of how to get back on the right path, or nervous about being accepted into the fold again.

In Jesus' parable of the lost sheep, He speaks of a shepherd who leaves his 99 sheep in search for the one that was lost. In the same way, our Good Shepherd is willing to go anywhere and everywhere looking for us when we lose our way. He does not want to see any of us miss out on the very best He has for us!

We don't have to stay lost. We don't have to stay separated from all of the goodness of God. No matter how far off we may have gotten, know that your Heavenly Father will go any distance to bring you back to Him.

Today, if you're feeling lost, call out to the Lord. Ask Him to refresh and renew your relationship — He will! Tap into courage and take the necessary steps to embrace all of the joy, life and healing that God has for your life. It doesn't matter how lost or misdirected you may feel right at this moment, God knows right where you are.

His help and blessings are ready as soon as you ask. He will lead and instruct you through "foreign territory." And the Holy Spirit will replace that lost and empty feeling with His joy and peace.

Romans 8:38-39 *"For I am convinced that neither death nor life, neither angels nor demons, neither the present nor the future, nor any powers, neither height nor depth, nor anything else in all creation, will be able to separate us from the love of God that is in Christ Jesus our Lord."*

PRAYER POINT

Father God, thank You that You have promised to guide me always, not just when I am up and on track. Today, I lean hard on this promise and ask You to continue to show me the way to walk.

Father, there are times when I feel like a sun-scorched land, but You promise to meet my needs even there. Today I acknowledge that I need You. I am parched and I look to You to give me emotional strength, spiritual insight and physical stamina. You even promise to strengthen my frame. Thank you Father that Your tender care encompasses all of me. Help me to draw on that today and to praise You for it!

Like David, You are my Shepherd, and I pray his prayer over my life:

¹The LORD is my shepherd, I lack nothing. ²He makes me lie down in green pastures, He leads me beside quiet waters, ³He refreshes my soul. He guides me along the right paths for his name's sake. ⁴Even though I walk through the darkest valley, I will fear no evil, for you are with me; Your rod and your staff, they comfort me. ⁵You prepare a table before me in the presence of my enemies. You anoint my head with oil; my cup overflows.⁶Surely your goodness and love will follow me all the days of my life, and I will dwell in the house of the LORD forever. Amen.

BREAKING OFF DOUBT

"Let's pray for her."

"Oh, I doubt she can be healed."

"We are moving forward."

"Oh, I doubt you can do it."

Doubt is an insidious little character. It capitalizes on every single opportunity it is given to eat away at dreams, hopes, and visions. If allowed, it will tear down the most certain of promises, leaving nothing left to build on. If you can think of it, doubt can crush it.

It's up to you to keep a steady watch and break the power of doubt at every turn. Entertaining doubt and the questions it offers can send you spiraling down a path that ends in questioning God's promises to you, His destiny for you, and a total lack of fulfillment in your Christian walk.

Even Jesus was faced with the powers of doubt when He was tempted in the wilderness. Jesus knew that there was no way that He could work miracles, cast out demons, and heal the sick if there was any doubt in His mind. He also knew that he could not preach with strong authority if doubt felt comfortable enough to whisper lies into His ear.

How much power does doubt have over you? Does doubt feel comfortable enough to take up residence in your mind? How do you handle doubt when it tries to whisper in your ear?

The Word of God says that we have to strengthen our minds and seriously set up roadblocks to the onslaught of doubt. From the way we live our lives, the words that come out of our mouths, to the thoughts that we entertain, we have to stay in faith, believe God's Word and actively keep doubt at bay.

Remember Philippians 4:13 *"I can do all things through Christ who strengthens me!"* You don't have to understand how you can do it. It's Christ's strength that's going to make it happen, so stop doubting. Believe that it's going to happen!

So, bottom line:

Do Christians doubt? Of course we do. But this does not mean we don't believe. You may be at 63%, 95%, or 51%, but know that with God, you are 100%. He is with you and will hold you tight.

PRAYER POINT

Dear Lord, I praise you for Your goodness to me! I am so grateful for Your timing in revealing the deliverance from doubt that I so needed! What a difference your Word and Your promises and strength have made for me! I rejoice in Your goodness to me!

I break off every spirit of doubt, fear and discouragement, in the name of Jesus. I close any place of entrance to doubt or fear and seal it with the blood of Christ. Let the promises in Your Word and the testimonies of Your faithfulness in my life and my friends' lives encourage my faith. I declare that I am bold and courageous in my faith. Because I know that I am loved by God, I choose to believe that His promises are for me. In the name of Jesus, Amen.

GOD'S FAVOR IS LAVISH!

Lavish: abundant; extravagant. To give in great amounts without limits.

God wants to lavish you with His love and favor in every area of your life!

Psalm 5:12 *"Surely, LORD, You bless the righteous; You surround them with Your favor as with a shield."*

Psalm 30:5 *"For His anger lasts only a moment, but His favor lasts a lifetime…"*

Did you get that last verse? God's favor is yours for your whole lifetime!

It is the time to determine that you are going to become more "favor minded": believing that the favor of God is for you, every day. You can expect raises in your pay and promotions even when there are no raises and no promotions being given in your company because you have God's favor through Christ Jesus.

You cannot predict when or how this favor will show up; you can only have faith that it will! It is time. It is the set time for the Lord to unlock all manner of favor on you right now; not just a little favor, but an abundance of favor. God is lavish!

Second Corinthians 9:8 *"And God is able to bless you abundantly, so that in all things at all times, having all that you need, you will abound in every good work."*

Expect today to receive God's favor that is extravagant, beyond measure. It's your spiritual inheritance that heaven has given to you, as it is written in the Last Will and Testament of Jesus Christ called the New Testament. This inheritance is so important to us; I believe this is why Peter and Paul ended their letters to the churches with praying for God's favor and peace to be multiplied to them.

Second Peter 1:2 *"Grace and peace be yours in abundance through the knowledge of God and of Jesus our Lord."*

So I close today's "Pep Talk" with a blessing for you: That the grace and the favor of God and His peace be multiplied to you now, in Jesus' Name.

Make this confession your daily prayer and begin to expect God's favor in your life.

PRAYER POINT

Heavenly Father, I declare that I have Your favor today. I declare that I am strong and well able to fulfill my God given destiny; I know that You are fighting my battles for me.

I declare that I am a victor and not a victim. I may have been defeated in the past but the past is past: this is new day.

Your Word says that "I am the head and not the tail" and "I will lend and I will not borrow." Everything I touch will prosper and succeed according to your perfect will because of Your favor, Father.

I declare that by Your stripes I am healed today. I will live and not die. I declare that You are restoring my health, and with long life You satisfy me.

Father, today I declare Your favor in my relationship with You; favor in my relationship with my spouse and my family; favor in relationships with my friends; and favor in relationships in my business. I want to thank You for causing me to be at the right place at the right time.

I want to thank You for causing people to want to help me.

Today, Father I want to thank You for blessing me with creativity, I want to thank You for causing me to make good decisions with a clear mind.

I declare that You are smiling down on me today and that Your favor will be in everything I do because I am pleasing to You. I declare that I will be blessed in the city and blessed in the country, blessed coming in and blessed going out.

I claim Psalm 84:11 right now, that You are blessing me with favor and honor and no good thing will You withhold from me because my walk is blameless.

I claim Habakkuk 2:3, that my dream and my vision is for an appointed time. Though it may tarry, I will earnestly wait for it, for it will surely come.

I declare today that I am filled with Your "can do" power. Father, between You and me, we are the majority and I can do all things through Christ who strengthens me.

I know that Your Word says that, "no man has seen, heard or even imagined the wonderful things that You have in store for those that love You" and I want to tell you that I love You and I want to thank You for loving me.

I want to thank you for Your favor today, not because of who I am, but because of whose I am. I am a child of the Most High God, the Creator of the whole universe.

I walk in the favor and the blessing of the Lord every day of my life. The favor of God goes with me and produces success in my life! The favor of God opens doors for me that no man can shut. The favor of God is manifesting every day in my life!

By the favor of God, I will not be defeated but rather enjoy victory after victory! The favor of God is on my life and the enemy never triumphs over me! Others recognize the favor of God on my life. God's favor is overtaking my life no matter where I live, no matter the economy of my nation or the world and no matter where I go in the earth! This is my set time for God's favor.

I commit this day of favor to You.

In Jesus' name, Amen

> Lying in bed reading —this truth hit me —If you think women are the weaker sex, try pulling the blankets back to your side.

STOP BEING A VICTIM

I woke up early one morning with these words on my mind, "If you have been hurt by someone and are still carrying the pain and hurt, it is time to put a stop to it." As long as you insist on dwelling and feeling the pain of abuse, hurt, divorce, trauma, negative words, or an unkind parent you will never feel peace and victory in your life.

You must release that thing—it is like a cancer that keeps eating away. Forgive the person or persons who hurt you. Release yourself and break the curse of bondage over your life.

(Romans 8:37) *No, in all these things we are more than conquerors through Him who loved us.*

This may sound strange to some of us, the truth is that sometimes it is comfortable to be a victim. Some people grow used to feeling sorry for themselves, throwing pity parties, and inviting others to join in: "You poor thing! You really have it rough!" We all enjoy a little pity once in a while.

Being a victim also comes in handy when we don't feel like changing. We might blame our troubled childhood, our alcoholic spouse, our nasty boss, or our painful illness. After all, who can expect us to move ahead in life? Don't we have every right to wallow in self-pity?

Jesus shatters the victim mentality. We are tempted to think of ourselves as helpless lambs being dragged to the slaughter. But faith in Jesus makes us *"more than conquerors through Him who loved us."* Nothing, no matter how painful or powerful, can separate us from God's love in Christ Jesus. That makes us victorious, no matter what.

One of my greatest joys as a pastor has been in seeing God's love overcome the victim mentality. People paralyzed by pain and self-pity discover how much God loves them. They find that Christ's riches are greater than their problems, that a victory celebration is more fun than a pity party. They stop using their troubles as an excuse, and they overcome them. Through God's love, they become more than conquerors, and so can you.

Set into motion God's blessings! I was there years ago, but today I am free. It took a specific decision on my part. Once I declared and believed that greater is Christ in me than the enemy in this world, I was free. The chains came off. Stop feeling sorry for yourself and get over it! The best of your life is ahead of you. Your children or your future children will inherit your freedom and not the curses of abuse when you make that decision for yourself today! Praise God!

PRAYER POINT

Jesus, My Savior and victory, show us the riches of Your salvation. Help us to receive and enjoy Your benefits and give You all praise. Father, today I set into motion Your New Covenant promises. I declare that no weapon formed against me or my family will prosper.

I decree that no evil, sickness, accidents, interruptions, lack, poverty, robberies, fear, sudden death, pestilence, mind attacks, lies, temptations, or insatiable desires (ravenous, unappeasable, cravings, addictive desires), will come near me or affect my life and my loved ones.

I declare that I am the righteousness of God in Christ Jesus. I declare that greater is Christ in me than the enemy in this world. I declare that the Holy Spirit is guiding me and instructing me and my loved ones in all our ways. I declare that my spouse is growing in Christ and is full of your wisdom, knowledge, and understanding to be all that you have created him/her to be.

The Word of God is a lamp that shines on my feet and a light that illuminates my path—every step I take (Proverbs 6:23; Psalm.27:1).

I declare that today I walk in Your fullness, guided by the Holy Spirit, and hedged around and about by the protection of your angelic hosts. I declare that I have the mind of Christ and today I will make wise decisions and prosperous investments.

Thank you Father, Lord Jesus, and Holy Spirit for supplying everything I need today. Keep me from all temptations and procrastination (laziness, putting things off, unfinished business).

In Jesus Christ's name, Amen.

> **Thank coffee for tricking us into believing that it's a good morning for a few minutes.**

GIVE GOD PRAISE

I am going to actively give God praise in the midst of this hard place, and I am going to choose to have the joy of the Lord. The Bible says rain falls on the just and on the unjust. Christians suffer just like non-believers this side of heaven. Living in a fallen world, we're destined to trek through valleys. However, many promises in the Bible point to God not letting the faithful suffer unnecessarily or for an indefinite period of time (though it feels like it at times).

James 1:12 *Blessed is the one who perseveres under trial because, having stood the test, that person will receive the crown of life that the Lord has promised to those who love Him.*

Some people appear to suffer more trials than others, or more than what seems fair. I don't have an answer for that, except to say God is sovereign and we have to trust Him to do the right thing. He supplies all our needs, which may look different than we expect.

God is still on His throne. More importantly, He's on the throne of my heart and never once has He deserted me.

Does it feel like God has deserted you? Consider this for a moment: the toughest thing God asks is for us to die to self and be willing to sacrifice everything for Him. But hear what I'm saying—that doesn't mean He will always take it.

In the Biblical story of Abraham, he waited his entire adult life for a son. What did God ask of him? Put Isaac on the altar. God had no intention of taking Isaac, but He wanted Abraham's whole heart and obedience.

God points to whatever our "Isaac" is and says, "Lay it on the altar." It's difficult to do when we can't see the end result.

God honors obedience. This doesn't mean we can't cry out to God, even when we have no words to express our pain and outrage (Romans 8:26), He can take it! God will never forsake you.

We have a choice. We can go through life with God or without Him. I don't know about you, but I'd hate to try to live in this world without Him, regardless of what He asks me to endure. I need His comfort. When I can't trust what the world hands me, I can trust Him.

PRAYER POINT

Lord, I thank You that when I am weak or frightened, I choose to delight in You!

> Psalm 37:23-24 *²³The Lord makes firm the steps of the one who delights in Him; ²⁴though he may stumble, he will not fall, for the Lord upholds him with his hand.*

I give You praise for keeping me safe throughout this week.

> Second Samuel 22:2-3 *²The Lord is my rock, my fortress and my deliverer; my God is my rock, in whom I take refuge, my shield and the horn of my salvation. ³He is my stronghold, my refuge and my savior - from violent people you save me.*

Even though my mind is concerned, my heart is fixed on the promises of Your Word.

> John 14:27 *Peace I leave with you; my peace I give you. I do not give to you as the world gives. Do not let your hearts be troubled and do not be afraid.*

Though I may feel isolated and alone today, I am never without Him!

> Hebrews 13:5 *Never will I leave you; never will I forsake you.*

Despite those things that have taken place, my life overflows with Your blessings.

> Philippians 4:11 *I have no reason to complain. I have learned, in whatsoever state I am, to be content.*

Even though it seems like I will be overwhelmed, You will never allow me to crumble beneath the weight of it all.

> Second Corinthians 4:8-9 *⁸We are hard pressed on every side, but not crushed; perplexed, but not in despair; ⁹persecuted, but not abandoned; struck down, but not destroyed.*

Thank You so much for helping me to notice that You are active and in control no matter the storm clouds.

> Psalm 138:7 *Though I walk in the midst of trouble, you preserve my life. You stretch out your hand against the anger of my foes; with your right hand you save me.*

I give You praise for Your ever-renewing mercies and grace.

> Hebrews 4:16 *Let us then approach God's throne of grace with confidence, so that we may receive mercy and find grace to help us in our time of need.*

Whew! I feel better already. How about you? In spite of it all, we always have a reason to give God thanks!

KEEPING ME SAFE

Outside my front window, I saw four children playing hide and seek. I had to laugh at some of their funny hiding places. Many decades ago I played that game. Into my mind flashed hiding places that felt cozy enough to sleep in while others were cramped, cold and hard. This sounds like some of the challenging places God assigns to His children today.

My hiding place in God—the place or circumstance where He keeps me safe in Him—may not always be comfortable by my finite human standard. Whether pleasant or painful for the moment, it fits His plan for my growth, ministry and protection. Because He drew me to Himself and saved me through the Cross, He will continue to guide and train me. He always does, in His chosen places.

My King may use any part of His creation to keep me in His presence. By hiding rebellious Jonah three days in the belly of a great fish, He provided safety from the sea. This is proof of His sovereignty, and the personal humbling needed for Jonah to follow God's command.

By hiding Israel in Egypt—in 400 grueling years of slavery—God unified His people and guarded them from the rising corruption in Canaan, their ultimate destination.

I trust that He will always choose the hiding place for me that best prepares me for tomorrow's challenges. It may not look or feel like a hiding place designed by my Father's wise and loving hand but as I rest in Him, He will accomplish His purpose.

Psalm 37:23-24 *The LORD makes firm the steps of the one who delights in Him; though he may stumble, he will not fall, for the LORD upholds him with his hand.*

I give you praise for keeping me in safety throughout this week. He said: *"The LORD is my rock, my fortress and* my deliverer; my God is my rock, in whom I take refuge, my shield and the horn of my salvation. He is my stronghold, my refuge and my savior, from violent people you save me"* (2 Samuel 22:2-3).

Even though my mind is concerned, my heart is fixed on the promises of Your Word. *Peace I leave with you; my peace I give you. I do not give to you as the world gives. Do not let your hearts be troubled and do not be afraid* (John 14:27).

Hebrews 13:5 *Keep your lives free from the love of money and be content with what you have, because God has said, "Never will I leave you; never will I forsake you.*

Despite those things that I still desire, my cup overflows with your blessings. *I am not saying this because I am in need, for I have learned to be content whatever the circumstances* (Philippians 4:11).

2 Corinthians 4:8-9 *We are hard pressed on every side, but not crushed; perplexed, but not in despair; persecuted, but not abandoned; struck down, but not destroyed.*

Thank You so much for helping me to notice the silver linings of the storm clouds. *Though I walk in the midst of trouble, you preserve my life. You stretch out your hand against the anger of my foes; with your right hand you save me* (Psalm 138:7).

I give You praise that the rain is only helping me to grow and develop the character that You want me to have. *And the God of all grace, who called you to his eternal glory in Christ, after you have suffered a little while, will Himself restore you and make you strong, firm and steadfast* (1 Peter 5:10).

Most of all, thank You Lord for forgiving me of my many shortcomings and mistakes. I give You praise for Your ever-renewing mercies and grace.

Let us then approach God's throne of grace with confidence, so that we may receive mercy and find grace to help us in our time of need (Hebrews 4:16).

Whew! I feel better already. How about you? In spite of it all, we still have a reason to give God thanks!

PRAYER POINT

Dear God,

I want to thank You for what You have already done. I am not going to wait until I see results or receive rewards. I am thanking You right now! I am not going to wait until I feel better or things look better. I am thanking You right now.

I am not going to wait until people say they are sorry or until they stop talking about me. I am thanking You right now. I am not going to wait until the pain in my body disappears. I am thanking You right now. I am not going to wait until my financial situation improves. I am going to thank You right now.

I am not going to wait until the children are asleep and the house is quiet. I am going to thank You right now. I am not going to wait until I get promoted at work or until I get the job. I am going to thank You right now. I am not going to wait until I understand every experience in my life that has caused me pain or grief. I am going to thank You right now.

I am not going to wait until the journey gets easier or the challenges are removed. I am thanking You right now.

I am thanking You because I am alive.

I am thanking You because I made it through the day's difficulties.

I am thanking You because I have walked around the obstacles.

I am thanking You because I have the ability and the opportunity to do more and do better.

I'm thanking You Father, because You have not given up on me.

God is just so good, and He's good all the time.

In Your Son Jesus Christ's precious and Holy Name I pray,

Amen.

> The Swiss must've been pretty confident in their chances of victory if they included a corkscrew in their army knife.

YOU WIN!

Lindy and I love movies. I love the crucial scene in "The Lion King" when Scar had Simba hanging over a cliff, or the one scene in "The Matrix" when Neo appeared to be dead. All of these characters were at their breaking point. They were fighting their ultimate enemy and seemingly failing.

Right now if you are in a battle, maybe it feels like the ultimate fight. You are facing your greatest trial and it seems like all is lost. Before you give in, let me remind you: you are more than a conqueror! You are a child of the great God! You were made in His image and likeness. He gave you the keys to the Kingdom. He gave you power over the enemy. Use it!

Don't believe the hype! Don't believe the lies that the devil is whispering. If you have to close your eyes to how it looks, shut them tight! Hang in there! If God is for you, who can be against you?

You have to believe God's Word and stand firm. Grit your teeth and remember that at your greatest point of pressure, you are about to receive your greatest breakthrough. If you give in, you will never taste the thrill of victory and will have to settle for defeat. Why settle when God has already told you that you are going to win?

Time and space are powerless against the Christian because whatever life brings, the love of God triumphs over it. No angelic power of any sort can separate us from God, There is nothing you can think of that can separate us from God's love for us. Life, death, angels, demons, or all of them combined cannot separate us from His love.

This wonderful love, from which we cannot be separated, is the love of God that is in Christ Jesus our Lord.

It can be experienced only in Christ Jesus. God demonstrated that majestic sacrificial love at Calvary.

Yes, believers are all super-conquerors, more than conquerors in Jesus Christ. We are "super-overcomers" in Christ by His enabling grace. So, jump back over the cliff like Simba. Find a way to breathe again like Neo. Keep on fighting! You are the hero in the story of your life! You will win!

Romans 8:37 *No, in all these things we are more than conquerors through Him who loved us.*

Dear friend, I know our God is not only a God of near, but of far too! Distance doesn't matter for Him! His words will never come back without finishing the purpose for which it has been sent! So, relax and rejoice for the joy of the LORD is our strength! Take care and stay blessed! God be with you in all that you do for His glory!

PRAYER POINT

Lord, we thank You and praise You for all that You have been doing in our lives! We know that You are able to fulfill every need according to Your riches in glory! Wipe away our tears and clothe us with the joy of Your salvation! We commit all the areas of our lives into Your loving care! Guard us, guide us, protect us and bless us! I speak breakthrough in all the areas of our lives in the name of Jesus Christ!

Let your blood cover our household. I speak divine healing in the name of Jesus Christ! Fill my home with your peace that passes all understanding! Deliver my home from all bondage and curses! I pray and receive all that I have asked for and all that you have for me and my family through the name of our Lord and Savior, Jesus Christ!

Amen!

> There is nothing more annoying than two people talking while you're trying to interrupt.

It's a New Day

INTRODUCTION

Each year—as the New Year approaches—we make resolutions for the coming year. Each resolution differs from person to person. Some can be life-altering, such as going back to school, losing weight or finding love. Some can even be as simple as making more time for family and spending less time on things we feel we put too much time into.

Whatever it may be, remember that God is also aware of every plan we make. When we place more focus on seeking His thoughts, approval and guidance on each resolution, it works for our better more often than not.

God has long range goals and plans for each of us. His will is for us to be happy, healthy and full of His Spirit. IT IS A NEW DAY!

His will is for us to grow and not be stagnant. IT IS A NEW DAY!!

His plans are for our betterment in each area that we are concerned about. By relying on Him and the leading of the Holy Spirit, we will succeed in the long run even if we feel we have failed. In truth, what we may consider a loss can be a success in another area of our lives, even if it's spiritual or character growth!

At Proverbs 16:3, we read *Commit to the LORD whatever you do, and He will establish your plans.* In Psalms 37:3-4, we also read *Trust in the LORD and do good; dwell in the land and enjoy safe pasture. Take delight in the LORD, and He will give you the desires of your heart.*

Introduction

WOW! IT REALLY IS A NEW DAY!

Over the past few years, Lindy and I have endured a lot of trials and stretching. I can bear testimony to the tough part of waiting on the Lord and of having to have sole reliance on His will and not on my own. The past several months have taught me to be grateful for small blessings that come each day. After much perseverance, God will make a way even when there doesn't seem to be a way! IT IS A NEW DAY! In "cultivating faithfulness," we grow. It is through this that we are blessed!

As we look forward, another verse that comes to mind is Jeremiah 29:11 where we read this promise and assurance, *"For I know the plans I have for you," declares the LORD, "plans to prosper you and not to harm you, plans to give you hope and a future."*

His plans for us are established already by having faith in His will for the coming years! Each of us have a promise that the coming days and months can be our best yet! Those plans may be different for each of us, but with God behind us, how can we fail? Romans 8:31 says, *What, then, shall we say in response to these things? If God is for us, who can be against us?"*

I pray that each of us will have blessed "NEW DAYS." That each of us will continue to grow in grace and faith and that all of our heart's desires will be blessed.

Remember to seek His will and cultivate faithfulness as you wait. By doing so, you will find that things work for your good as we read this promise in Romans 8:28 *And we know that in all things God works for the good of those who love Him, who have been called according to His purpose.*

FINDING GOD!

I admire Nicodemus the Pharisee. He was able to recognize that God was working through Jesus after observing His ministry to the people. Nicodemus saw that Jesus would not have been able to perform the miracles He did without the help of God.

Jesus' ministry was a radical ministry. It wasn't built on rules or traditions like what the Jews were practicing at the time. Its foundation was love and forgiveness. Jesus didn't view God as apart or aloof from man, but He regarded the Lord as His Father—someone with whom He could have a close relationship with. Jesus performed miracles that boggled the mind and told His followers that they could do the same.

Many learned men who witnessed Jesus' ministry chose to ignore the glory and focus on what they knew. They knew Scripture. They knew tradition. They knew the rules of man. Jesus was out of the box. He didn't line up with what they knew.

So instead of seeing God working in Him, they chose to see how Jesus didn't fit. They chose to focus on how Jesus was out of line with tradition and their rules. They missed that Jesus was creating a whole new space of love and grace.

But Nicodemus recognized that God was moving in a new way and he came to Jesus to get answers. He came to Jesus to fill in the blanks. The resulting conversation is the cornerstone to our salvation ministry.

I love that God can use new and different things for His glory. He uses foolish things to confound the wise. Though He always remains the same, the Lord uses ways we could never imagine to display His glory and love.

Many of the Pharisees in Nicodemus' day missed out on recognizing who Jesus was. They were so caught up in what they believed to be correct that they missed when the answer to their greatest prayers showed up on their doorstep.

Do not allow your preconceived notions about what it means to be a Christian, what ministry looks like, or how you think things should be keep you from experiencing an encounter with God. Don't dismiss something as unholy just because it's not done in the way you think it should be done.

Look beyond what you know and seek the presence of the Lord. You may be surprised how He has chosen to reveal Himself.

John 3:1-2 *Now there was a Pharisee, a man named Nicodemus who was a member of the Jewish ruling council. He came to Jesus at night and said, "Rabbi, we know that you are a teacher who has come from God. For no one could perform the signs you are doing if God were not with him."*

PRAYER POINT

Our Father, may everything I do begin with Your inspiration, continue with Your help and reach perfection under Your Guidance.

With Your loving care, guide me in my daily actions. Help me to persevere with love and sincerity. Teach me to judge wisely the things of earth and to love the things of Heaven.

Keep me in Your presence and never let me be separated from You.
Your Spirit made me Your child, so I can confidently call You Father.

Make Your Love the foundation of my life.
Teach me to long for Heaven.
May its promise and hope guide my way on earth
May Your Kingdom come! Amen

> I may not be the smartest guy in the world, or the richest guy in the world, or the best looking guy in the world, ...Oh heck, now I'm depressed.

BENEFITS OF EMPOWERMENT

As a child of the King, you now have an incredible inheritance, a big part of which is available in this life. At birth, God gives each of us natural gifts such as artistic, musical, athletic or intellectual abilities. However, after you become a believer, God also gave you supernatural, miracle-working gifts. The complete set of nine supernatural gifts is listed in First Corinthians 12.

When you were born again, you were given the authority of a son or daughter of the King, the Most High God. The Bible says all authority was given to Jesus (Matthew 28:18). Jesus Himself said that He gave supernatural authority to His followers (Luke 10:19) so they might do the works He did (John 14:11-12). YOU HAVE BEEN EMPOWERED!

The Benefits of Empowerment:

<u>Passion for God</u> – You will have an increased hunger for God and all the things of God. You will move into deeper levels of prayer and worship. You will better understand God's nature, personality, power and Word.

<u>Passion of God</u> – You will begin to be much more concerned about the things God is most concerned about. God will give you His concern for the lost. He will even give you love and compassion for people you don't even know. You will have a new compassion for the hurting and wounded.

<u>Power of God</u> – You will immediately begin to experience God's supernatural power in your life. Large and small miracles will begin to occur in your life and in the lives of those you pray for as you walk in the power of the Holy Spirit.

Sensitivity to God – You will develop a higher level of receptivity to the leading of the Holy Spirit and become much more aware of God's divine intervention and angelic activity around you. You will talk to God and will actually hear Him communicate back to you in a variety of ways.

John spoke of this glorious inheritance in First John 3:1-3: *See what great love the Father has lavished on us, that we should be called children of God! And that is what we are! The reason the world does not know us is that it did not know Him. Dear friends, now we are children of God, and what we will be has not yet been made known. But we know that when Christ appears, we shall be like Him, for we shall see Him as he is. All who have this hope in Him purify themselves, just as He is pure.*

Our challenge is to truly believe what the Scripture says, that we are co-heirs with Jesus Christ of everlasting life—which the resurrected Son of God has already inherited. Our inheritance is fantastic and we should constantly celebrate that we are co-heirs with Jesus Christ of all things that the Father has given Him!

Praise be to the God and Father of our Lord Jesus Christ, who has blessed us in the heavenly realms with every spiritual blessing in Christ. For He chose us in Him before the creation of the world to be holy and blameless in His sight. In love, He predestined us for adoption to son-ship through Jesus Christ, in accordance with His pleasure and will.

In Him, we were also chosen, having been predestined according to the plan of Him who works out everything in conformity with the purpose of His will, in order that we, who were the first to put our hope in Christ, might be for the praise of His glory. And you also were included in Christ when you heard the message of truth, the gospel of your salvation. When you believed, you were marked in Him with a seal, the promised Holy Spirit, who is a deposit guaranteeing our inheritance until the redemption of those who are God's possession – to the praise of his glory (Ephesians 1:3-5, 11-14).

Benefits of Empowerment

Give thanks to God for such a wonderful inheritance as heirs of God, and co-heirs with Jesus Christ.

PRAYER POINT

Dear Lord,

I thank You for saving and baptizing me with Your Holy Spirit. I ask that You now use me powerfully in your Kingdom, to bring Your light into the dark places. I pray as I walk in obedience to You and Your Word, that You will guide my every step.

I pray that You will give me faith, wisdom and the desires of my heart. Give me Your vision and show me Your plans for my life. I want to walk in Your blessings all the days of my life. I thank You for blessing my children and their children as they know You more.

In the mighty name of Jesus Christ, I pray.

Amen.

Stressed spelled backwards is *desserts*. Coincidence? I think not.

SHOULD'A, COULD'A, WOULD'A

I should'a done that when I had the chance!
That could'a been me, if I had gone to college!
I would'a been rich if I knew the people he knew!

"*Should'a, Could'a, and Would'a*" are a sneaky trio. They come sliding in to visit every now and then, whispering their groans about how you like: "Should'a done this," and "Could'a done that" and "if you would'a done something else, you'd be better off." They cluck their tongues and shake their heads disapprovingly at the current state of your life.

If we're not careful, we can find ourselves entertaining them by inviting them to have a seat in our minds. We let them stay awhile. Before we know it, we are in a depressed mood, lamenting the perfection that *Should'a, Could'a, and Would'a* been.

Sure, you might have missed a few opportunities. Perhaps if you would have done some things differently, you might be at a different spot. Don't let these three words take you hostage! Stand strong against their onslaught of disappointment and regret.

Every living person has regrets. "If only I worked harder on my project, I could have been promoted"…"If only I had said sorry, then my kids wouldn't hate me"…"If only I went to graduate school"…"if only I married him then I would be happy"…"if only, if only" sounds like, *Should'a, Could'a, Would'a!*

Do any of these 'if onlys' sound eerily familiar? As a Christian you are invited to walk in a life of freedom instead of living with the yoke of *Should'a, Could'a, Would'a!"*

This trio of thinking leads a person down the beaten path of guilt and into the pit of shame.

Guilt never strays too far away from us. It likes hanging around, waiting for the right moment to step in and finish us off. Feeling guilty does not mean that a person is, in fact, guilty. Feeling does not equal fact. When we battle with false guilt something in our reality is distorted. The distortion comes from a long list from that sickly trio *Should'a, Could'a, Would'a,* which always makes us feel like failures.

You cannot change your past. Today is what you have, and this day was made for you to rejoice in (Psalm 118:24)! Remember that the Lord is ordering your steps (Psalm 37:23). He is in full control. As long as you're following His lead, you can rest assured that you are in the perfect spot right now.

So, stop listening to *Should'a, Could'a, and Would'a!* Kick them out of your thoughts! Evict them out of the corners of your mind. Keep the Father, Son, and Holy Spirit as the primary residents of your soul instead, and watch what you accomplish moving forward!

Philippians 3:13-14 *Brothers and sisters, I do not consider myself yet to have taken hold of it. But one thing I do: Forgetting what is behind and straining toward what is ahead, I press on toward the goal to win the prize for which God has called me heavenward in Christ Jesus.*

PRAYER POINT

Dear Lord,

Help me not to miss the opportunities of learning, whether in school or life-lessons. Help me to study, to train, and to accept Your discipline; in doing so, I may deepen my life, enrich my mind, learn my trade, master my craft, be efficient in my job, and be equipped for my profession.

Help me never to miss the opportunities of helping others. May I be ready to share with the poor, to sympathize with the hurting, to encourage the depressed, to help those who made mistakes get back on track again, and to lend a hand to those who are finding things difficult.

Help me to never miss an opportunity to reveal who Christ in my life, by how I love others and do good. May I have courage to share the Good News of a loving God who heals the hurting, sets free the captive and makes the impossible possible.

So help me to take hold of every opportunity You send and to use every gift You have given me that I may make my life what You meant it to be.

Father of Life, thank You that You make all things new! May the power of your love be with me in everything I do.

Amen.

IT'S A NEW SEASON!

I love the Fall season! Kids are back in school, filling their brains with information they will someday need to rule the world and boss us around. Farmers are in the fields gathering a harvest that will put another inch on our waistlines this Winter. Leaves are beginning to blush with color and Jack Frost is whispering of howling things to come.

Yes, Summer has lost its grip and Autumn is here with burning leaves, kids in masks and turkeys hoping for a pardon from the president! There is something exciting about the change of seasons. It speaks of the passage of time in our lives. As always, there are old things to let go and new things upon which to lay hold.

While Spring speaks of renewal, Fall speaks not only of harvest, but of putting away and preparation. Just ask the squirrels. They know what's coming. Do you remember your grandmother's cellar lined with canned tomatoes, peaches, beans and an assortment of other culinary delights? I do! I still remember the smell of that dark cellar. Those sweet little ladies knew that summer's abundance must be preserved for winter's scarcity. All the work of cultivation in the summer's heat, the planting, the weeding, the watering, the fertilizing and the waiting eventually paid off in a bountiful harvest.

God is a gardener, too. He made a beautiful garden in which Adam and Eve could grow and reach their potential. Yep, He's got a green thumb for sure! We've all read John 15 and know about His love for fruit. Our hearts are His soil where He plants His crops of love, joy, peace, patience, kindness, goodness, faithfulness, gentleness and self-control. He knows winter is coming and preparations must be made ahead of time. The world is starving and just the right jar off His shelf at just the right time will be what someone needs when life's winds are no longer warm, gentle and filled with the fragrance of roses.

Someone you will meet soon may be in the winter of their life. They try to mask their hunger. Having experienced a winter season, you know the signs of starvation - that gaunt look with the empty eyes. Before that, God had pruned you, weeded your life, and laid some smelly fertilizer around your rooted feet. You thought He was being cruel, but He was thinking ahead. He harvested you and set you on a shelf. You thought He forgot all about you there in that dark cellar. No. The waiting also had a purpose. Now, the one with the gaunt look is standing in front of you needing a taste of what God has done in your life.

We know God is good but will that person be able to "taste and see that the Lord is good" in us? Did anything spoil the canning and preservation process? Did air, mold and bacteria break the seal of the Spirit and find a way in to spoil the sweet fruit? Was the nutritional value lost because of bitterness or unforgiveness?

It's harvest time and the farmer's work isn't complete until everything is preserved for future need. Will you allow God to prepare and preserve you? Will you submit to purifying fire and lonely isolation? Will you remember that God does all things well and His timing is perfect even when He leaves you to sit on the shelf?

It's a new season and a new day. The things that God has done in us will be used when the time is right. Don't fear the changes that come with season change. It's needed for God to accomplish His goal. Difficult times may be ahead - if not for you, for someone else and God is doing now what must be done to prepare us for the bitterness of winter's scarcity. While many have to struggle without provision, God has a cellar full of abundance that will be just what is needed when summer's bounty is a distant memory.

Psalm 23:5 says, *You prepare a table before Me in the presence of my enemies.* How sweet to know that in the midst of winter, in the midst of the wilderness, even in the presence of my enemies, God can prepare a table that is full and overflowing.

PRAYER POINT

God of the Harvest, by whose Holy Spirit all things are made new, I praise You for the gift of life, for the blessing of a new season, for the mercy that makes each day a fresh start.

Give me grace for each season that comes my way. Let me see the good fruit that is in me now. I long to to experience Your Presence daily, and to know the hope that comes from being made new in Christ.

In His name I pray,

Amen.

> At 60 it just dawned on me that education is a funny thing. At eighteen we know all the answers--forty years later even the questions confuse us.

A GREAT DAY TO DAYDREAM!

God and I want to encourage you to start dreaming again with His dreams— no matter what is going on in the world, no matter what has happened in your past, no matter what is happening in your life right now and no matter what it looks like could happen in your future.

I want you to know that God is bigger than all the stuff that tries to stop you from moving forward in your life, including the family you were born into, lack of education, the spouse you are married to, health issues, financial problems, or the lack of opportunities.

My answer is Jesus Christ. Jesus is your guarantee of a better today and a much better tomorrow. That is why you can dare to start dreaming again.

Think about this: as a Christian, you are a new man in Christ Jesus and it is from this perspective that you can dare to dream again. Realizing that you were crucified with Him, were buried with Him and rose again with Him in newness of life is your guarantee of God given dreams becoming reality in your life. He has given you abundant life to the fullest, until it overflows into living your God-given dreams.

God has made you a dreamer like Himself, for you were created in His likeness and image. Being a dreamer is your God nature in Christ Jesus, so you are no little person in your spirit. God has made you a dreamer so that you would not be hopeless; instead, you will live an extraordinary life. Dreamers are people who can see things that others cannot see and are the most powerful people on the earth.

What are God Dreams?

- God-given dreams are God's dreams, God's hopes, God's desires, and God's plans for you that are already planned out and ready for you to discover and live.

- God-given dreams come from God and are spoken to your spirit. They are different from simple, flimsy wishes, for they capture your thoughts, your feelings, your emotions, your imagination and your spirit.

- God-given dreams show you how God sees you and how He wants you to see yourself.

- God-given dreams are something you will embrace and they will embrace you.

- God-given dreams come to you in a single moment, yet they consume your thinking for a long time.

- God-given dreams are something you won't be able to set aside, for they will consume your thoughts, bring excited expectation of their fulfillment and stir a passion inside you to see them become reality in your life.

- God-given dreams stir your imagination and bring you into an expectant hope of living in those dreams.

- God-given dreams require you to become a dreamer - a big dreamer!

- God-given dreams are a testimony of the greatness of your God.

- God-given dreams require God's involvement to come to fulfillment. You weren't meant to do it alone.

PRAYER POINT

Father,

I once had such big dreams and so much anticipation of the future. Now, no shimmering horizon beckons me; my days are lackluster and I see so little of lasting value in my daily routine. Where is Your plan for my life? You have told us that without vision, we perish. So Father in heaven, release me from my bonds, and let me dream with You. Let me have vision for the impossible because then it will require You. Let me dream of what my life could be when I walk with You.

Along with the dream, will You give me supernatural grace and enduring strength to see the dream through to fruition? I sense that this may involve adventures I have not bargained for. I admit to liking some of my ruts, but I know that habit patterns that seem cozy nests from the inside may be prison cells from Your vantage point. But I want to trust You enough to follow, even if you lead along new paths.

In joyous expectation,

Amen.

> I hate it when I'm in a crowded elevator and yell out "GROUP HUG!" and people look at me all weird and stuff... Making friends is hard.

TODAY IS YOUR DAY!

It's a new day! You are in a new place, facing something you've never faced before. You have the opportunity to do something new, achieve something you never have before, or go somewhere you've never gone. God woke you up on purpose this morning. This is your day to fulfill something new for His Kingdom. It's up to you to get with Him and figure out just what that is. Don't think of today as just any ordinary day.

Philip was sharing the gospel and bringing souls into the Kingdom when an angel spoke to him and interrupted his flow. Philip's obedience to the angel led him to a man of great influence who he led to the Lord. When Philip's work was done, he was caught up in the spirit to a whole different city! (Acts 8:29-40)

Who knows what God wants to do with you today? Perhaps this is your day for an angelic visitation! Today is your day to receive new and wonderful blessings. Today could be your day to be a blessing. Today, a new door of promise could open. Today, your Kingdom purpose will become clearer. No matter what—today is your day! Grab a hold of it, get with God, and make the most of these 24 hours.

God wants to build you up into a bigger, stronger person than you are just now. He has bigger plans for your life, a bigger vision, a bigger and greater dream than you could ever imagine. The Greek word for "build" is *oikodmeo meaning to edify, strengthen, develop someone's life through acts of love and encouragement, to construct and build him or her up.*

Expect greatness. Look for the miraculous. Anticipate with joy all that the Father has for you today! You're not sitting there breathing for nothing. The Holy Spirit and You are going to have a great day!

Psalm 89:15-16 *Blessed are those who have learned to acclaim you, who walk in the light of your presence, Lord. They rejoice in your name all day long; they celebrate your righteousness.*

Have a wonderful day!

PRAYER POINT

Dear God,

Today, bring a fresh revelation of my identity and purpose in you. May I be a catalyst for light and love, and bring inspiration to those around me. May I have the strength to stand tall in the face of conflict and the courage to speak my voice—even when I'm scared.

May I have the humility to follow my heart, and the passion to live my soul's desires. May I seek to know the highest truth and dismiss the gravitational pull of my lower self. May I be brave enough to hear my heart, to let it soften so that I may gracefully choose faith over fear.

Today is my day to surrender anything that stands between me and the destiny you have for me. May I be drenched in Your Holiness and engulfed by Your love.

Thank You for drawing me into Your Presence and experiencing your extravagant love, Amen.

A NEW OUTLOOK ON LIFE

How do you feel about your life? Is it worthwhile? Let's change the question: What would it take for you to feel that your life is worthwhile? What would have to happen to make you feel really positive about your life?

If you won the lottery, would that do it? If your marriage suddenly was all patched up, would that do it? If your kids began to make you proud or if you got a promotion, would that do it? What would it take for you to really feel positive about your life?

Now if that's the way you're thinking, then you'll probably never feel really positive about life because all the little pieces that must come together to make you positive about life will probably never be there.

Philippians 3:12-14 reads, *Not that I have already obtained all this, or have already been made perfect, but I press on to take hold of that for which Christ Jesus took hold of me. Brothers, I do not consider myself yet to have taken hold of it. But one thing I do: Forgetting what is behind & straining toward what is ahead, I press on toward the goal to win the prize for which God has called me heavenward in Christ Jesus.* And to think that Paul writes these words while in prison!

Now stop for a moment and ask yourself, "What is Paul trying to grab hold of?" Paul tells us in Philippians 3:10-11, *I want to know Christ — yes, to know the power of his resurrection and participation in his sufferings, becoming like him in his death, and so, somehow, attaining to the resurrection from the dead.*

There will be disappointments in life, but every day we get the adventure of moving forward in Him and the power of the Holy Spirit. I love the excitement of discovering His power in my life. If that is our goal, then Romans 8:28 is true: *And we know that in all things God works for the good of those who love Him, who have been called according to His purpose.*

The world says that the way to feel good about ourselves is by climbing the ladder of success—by making a lot of money, having influential friends, receiving a lot of awards, or by belonging to the right circles. But the Bible teaches us that we are to feel good about ourselves <u>because God loves us</u>. You are such a treasured person in God's sight that He gave His only Son to redeem you, and have a personal relationship with you. Think about that for a while. God wants to partner with you in all of your dreams and trials—<u>now</u>! It is this truth that changed my life.

In my times of prayer and meditation, God has been showing me new and innovative ideas to continue reaching out to and involving more Christians in exciting Kingdom ministries. I am excited that I have the opportunity to implement these new ideas and empower and encourage so many outstanding believers.

I also know that sometimes we can get into a bit of a routine in our service to the Lord. Our participation becomes like a habit and we perform our responsibilities like a machine. We can even let the fire that God lit in us die down to glowing embers, and we lose the zeal we originally had.

However, all of that complacency changes when we get into the presence of the Lord and allow Him to show us His vision and plans for every area of our lives. God has a way of making everything fresh, and His ultimate creative process can invigorate any situation.

A New Outlook on Life

I love how God can take the ordinary and make it extraordinary! Nothing is routine when God is involved. He is a supernatural God. He releases the supernatural into our circumstances and brings miraculous results. It is our responsibility to move with the Holy Spirit in the change, so that our lives can continue to thrive with vitality. After all, "Holy Spirit Variety" is the spice of life!

Take some time today to allow the Holy Spirit to breathe new life into you and into every area of your walk with Him. Allow Him to remind you of the call that you have, and open yourself to hearing His fresh, supernatural take on your circumstances. Let God quicken your spirit anew with His inspiration.

Isaiah 43:19 *See, I am doing a new thing! Now it springs up; do you not perceive it? I am making a way in the wilderness and streams in the wasteland.*

PRAYER POINT

Father,

I pray for a new outlook on my life and Your plans, both for me, for all of my friends and my family. I pray for Your supernatural strength to see us all through when life is the hardest and when times are good. Father, give us Your extravagant grace when life seems to throw us a curve, and when we are unsettled or upset.

I pray for Your wisdom and Your goodness to carry us through the day, both when life is the hardest and when times are good. Father, You promised in Your Word to never leave or forsake us. Pour out Your love in abundance and let me be empowered with Hope.

Father, I thank you for hearing my prayer. I thank You for Your Son Jesus who continually showers us with His love. Holy Spirit, thank You for Your encouragement when life is the hardest and when times are good.

In Jesus' name, Amen.

> One of the guys on my staff told me he missed being in high school so I took his lunch money and gave him a wedgie.

A SEASON OF HARVEST

We declare that it is a Season of Harvest now!

You are going to reap, to harvest, in the many fields in your community, your friends, your family. You have hung in there, you haven't given up when times were difficult. And now, it is the season of harvest.

Galatians 6:9 *So let's not get tired of doing what is good. At just the right time we will reap a harvest of blessing if we don't give up.*

You need to go back and look at all of those seeds that you have planted. When I say seeds, I'm not just talking about financial, although that will come to you as well. I'm talking about the seeds you have spread within the community; you have done so many things to help people, for that is the nature and heartbeat of God. That is worship.

God says because you have been about worship and praise, He is elevating you because you are what His kingdom is all about.

I hear the Lord say, *The Harvest Season is upon you this day, a season of abundance. There is a brand new anointing upon you this day; it's an abundance, abundance, and abundance.*

I hear Him say, "Well done, good and faithful servants! *You have fought a good fight, and now I, the King of Glory, am stepping in! I'm stepping in, and I'm giving you an overflowing abundance! I'm going to overflow in your finances, in your thinking, in your everything. I am going to overflow in everything you do and say!*

Overflow in finances? Yes!

Overflow in miracles? Yes!

Overflow in your marriage? Yes!

Isaiah 61:7 *Instead of shame and dishonor, you will enjoy a double share of honor. You will possess a double portion of prosperity in your land, and everlasting joy will be yours.*

No more shame! No more embarrassment! There is a harvest of everlasting joy; an abundant harvest in your children and your land! There is an anointing for a double portion today!"

Within this season, you will see promises fulfilled and dreams realized. You must believe in the unseen because God and His angelic host are at work on your behalf. God specializes in fulfilling dreams. It's your season, it's ripe; it is the right time!

2 Corinthians 5:18 *So we fix our eyes not on what is seen, but on what is unseen, since what is seen is temporary, but what is unseen is eternal.*

PRAYER POINT

So, join me in this declaration:

"I dedicate myself and this day to the Lord. Everything concerning my life, family, ministry, and finances will be fruitful in this Season of Harvest.

I take authority over every evil spirit working to hinder my God-given purpose. Every squatter that is on my property and possessions, I command you to get off now.

Psalms 91 is my portion. No weapon that is formed against us can prosper. I build myself up in my faith and put on the whole armor of God.

I declare Isaiah 61:10 over my family: *My children and grandchildren will be recognized and honored among the nations. Everyone will realize that they are a people the LORD has blessed."*

```
As a John Wayne
kind of guy -- I
fight evil wherever
it may be --
except in dark,
scary places.
```

Living With Great Joy!

INTRODUCTION

Whatever joy is... give me a bunch of it!

Undoubtedly, there is much confusion about that little, three-letter word "joy." Is it simply a deeper form of happiness? Is it the opposite of sadness or depression?

The secular perception of joy is "lasting happiness." However, the Bible interprets joy very differently. In fact, God commands His people to be full of joy (Psalms 37:4; Philippians 4:4). If joy were an emotion based upon circumstances, then that command would seem rather harsh and unrealistic. But our joy is rooted in God.

Our joy is something that is unaffected by circumstances. It is a state of mind and an orientation of the heart. Joy is deep. It is a settled state of contentment, confidence and hope.

Look at Philippians 1:3-5, 7-8 *I thank my God every time I remember you. In all my prayers for all of you, I always pray with joy because of your partnership in the gospel from the first day until now. It is right for me to feel this way about all of you, since I have you in my heart; for whether I am in chains or defending and confirming the gospel, all of you share in God's grace with me. God can testify how I long for all of you with the affection of Christ Jesus."*

Paul tells the Philippians that he has been praying for them. But he doesn't just pray, he prays with joy. And his joy comes "because of your partnership in the gospel." Paul's joy is a shared joy. This partnership is more than just

Introduction

spending time together... there is a unity, a joy, a purpose that is held in common.

Think about a great experience you've had? Perhaps it was the birth of a child. Maybe it was a great buck you got during hunting season. Maybe it was a great honor paid to you or a life-changing insight. Whatever the experience, I would venture to say that it was a joy that was made complete as you shared it with others. A shared joy is a deeper joy. It is not something that is isolated and individual, it is a joy we share with millions around the world and makes us part of a tremendous movement of God.

Also, we live joyfully because we really are on a "Great Adventure." We went white water rafting a few years ago. At first we got into the water and enjoyed maneuvering the boat in the current. We faced a couple of "little rapids" and really enjoyed them. But as the journey continued we faced some more fierce rapids. We found ourselves filled with joy and laughter. We would have missed the fun of the good rapids if we had gotten out of the water after the "little rapids."

The Christian life is like that. We miss out if we stop progressing. The initial stages of the faith are enjoyable but they are nothing compared with what God will introduce us to as we continue to travel with Him. We must "stay the course."

It is also a joy that is anchored in God's work and promise. We are confident of our eternal destiny not because of our goodness but because of His. Telling others that you are going to Heaven is not arrogance (unless you think you are going there because you are better than most people), it is a confident declaration based on God's promise.

The Christian joy is an adventure that involves growth taking place in our lives. As we grow in faith old prejudices are overcome, hurts of the past give way to the freedom that comes from forgiveness.. Our behavior looks more and more like Christ. And we find it easier to trust Him in the tough times. Christian joy deepens as the years go by.

And it all starts when we receive God's gift of salvation. This joy will not begin until we stop running away from God and run to Him. It starts when we stop trying to earn His favor and instead rest in His grace.

Joy is both an outcome of our relationship with the Lord and our source of strength for our obedience of Him (John 15). The joy of the Lord is our strength (Nehemiah 8:9). God desires for His people to be strong in Him so He graciously gives us joy as we cooperate with Him in our sanctification (Philippians 2:12-13). The joy of the Lord is the source of our fulfillment. As we experience fulfillment in the Lord this way, we work out our salvation in ever-increasing levels of refinement. Christ-likeness deepens for those who have determined in their heart to walk the walk by faith and live for God's glory alone.

So what is joy? A better question is, "What is the joy of the Lord?"

The fuel that drives the engine of our worshipping hearts is the joy of the Lord. Our worshipping hearts keep us focused on the Lord for our fulfillment. As we delight in Him, He grows us in grace. This is so much more than simply being religious. This is walking through every moment of everyday living for His glory. The joy of the Lord both empowers and grows from that process.

DO REAL CHRISTIANS LAUGH?

Does Your Face Need a Tune-Up?

Who said, *"If you're not allowed to laugh in heaven, I don't want to go there"*?

(Hint: It wasn't Mark Twain.) It was Martin Luther.

In Heaven, I believe our joy will often erupt in laughter. When laughter is prompted by what's appropriate, God always takes pleasure in it. I think Jesus will laugh with us, and His wit and joy-filled nature will be our greatest sources of endless laughter and delight.

Where did humor originate? Not with people, angels, or satan. God created all good things, including good humor. If God didn't have a sense of humor, human beings, as His image-bearers, wouldn't either. Of course, if God didn't have a sense of humor, we probably also wouldn't have aardvarks, baboons, platypuses, and giraffes, just to name a few. (You have to smile when you picture one of these, don't you?)

What are some ways we can live our lives with more laughter? Well, for one thing, most of us should stop taking ourselves so seriously. It is OK to spend some time just having fun and enjoyment!

Another step toward more laughter is to hang around happy people. Laughter really does seem to be contagious. Also, most of us need to simplify our lives and avoid getting bogged down with busyness. Being over-tired and over-stressed can quickly rob us of our joy.

As we learn to trust God in every area of our lives and allow His joy to fill us to overflowing, our lives will begin to reflect His love and joy to others. Our joy-filled lives attract those who don't know Him. How can we rejoice in the midst of difficult and painful circumstances? It is His joy that strengthens us and carries us through.

There is something so special about the laughter of dear friends. What sound do you hear when friends gather to eat and talk? Instead of harsh words or critical talk, may it be the sound of laughter.

PRAYER POINT

Father, help me to live in the fullness of Your Joy. May others see the joy of Jesus in me, so that they might want to meet the Joy Giver.

May the Lord fill our mouths with laughter today.

Every face and heart that is harboring sadness or downcast spirits, may the Lord come in and restore happiness and the joy of eternal salvation.

Every circumstance that has been causing us to cry for so long now, may the Lord bring healing and restoration. May the rain of God's blessings fall upon us and wash away all our tears. May He turn our mourning into dancing and our sorrow into testimonies of joy.

May the Lord speedily fulfill all the promises He has made in our lives, and cause many to come and rejoice with us.

In Jesus' name, Amen.

FOCUS ON YOUR BLESSINGS

If only you had more money, more time, more support, more opportunity — more, more, more — then you could really get started on moving forward in life and in expanding His Kingdom!

A mind set that refuses to believe that you have everything you need right now to start moving towards the purposes the Lord has written on your heart will keep you settling for less than the brilliance you are capable of.

How do you begin to discard the ties that keep you bound to mediocrity? Focus on Holy Spirit blessings, not the seeming limitations. Focus on the blessings you have, the blessing you are, and the blessings that your life will contribute to the lives of others.

In every situation we face, we can have a grateful attitude and a heart of joy because we choose to focus on our blessings rather than on our constraints. I choose to embrace life with a thankful, joy-filled heart that comes from seeing all that the Lord is doing in and through me today!

Ephesians 1:3 *Praise be to the God and Father of our Lord Jesus Christ, who has blessed us in the heavenly realms with every spiritual blessing in Christ.*

Ephesians 3:20-21 *Now to Him who is able to do immeasurably more than all we ask or imagine, according to his power that is at work within us, to Him be glory in the church and in Christ Jesus throughout all generations, forever and ever! Amen.*

So, today I am full of joy and thankful because:

- I am alive! God is good.
- I still have my health and strength.
- I have amazing family, friends and loved ones - I love you guys!
- I love what I do in life. So grateful.
- Jesus loves me. That sounds cliché', but it's really the most important thing of all.

What are you thankful for this week?

Psalm 136:1-3 Give thanks to the LORD, for he is good. His love endures forever. Give thanks to the God of gods. His love endures forever. Give thanks to the Lord of lords: His love endures forever.

PRAYER POINT

Father,

I am so thankful that You are my Jehovah Jireh. I thank You Lord that Your word promises me that You will never leave or forsake me. Lord, thank You for revelation of the abundant life You have promised me. I am blessed.

Holy Spirit, Renew my mind, my heart and my soul. Take those things that are spiritual hindrances out of my life. Holy Spirit, transform me into the image of Jesus. Take away those things that would cause me to destroy or delay any blessing that You would bring into my life. I surrender any unforgiveness that I may be harboring. I will no longer focus on the things that I don't have, but rather I will focus on You Lord. I am blessed by God.

Lord, I stand in faith today trusting that everything I need and desire according to Your Will shall come to pass. I align myself to Your Kingdom plans and purposes for my life. I trust the timing for open doors and opportunities that you have planned. My steps are blessed by the Lord.

I command Satan to loose me right now and I cancel any assignment that he is planning. I take comfort in knowing that my blessings may be delayed but they are not denied! I can't wait to see what You are going to do in my life as I pursue Your Kingdom reign. I call my blessings down from heaven in the name of Jesus! I thank You and praise You for who You are and for being The Great I Am! I am blessed beyond measure.

Thank You for blessing me and for the outrageous blessings that are to come.

In the Mighty Name of Jesus Christ.

Amen.

```
This morning I found
myself starring at an
orange juice container
because it reads
concentrate.
```

HOLD TIGHTLY TO YOUR JOY

Do not allow the enemy to steal your joy!

Hanging on to the joy of the Lord is not always easy. Satan wants to rob you of this incredible, God-given treasure. He will do everything in his power to steal it away, making your unhappy experience even worse.

Jesus said in John 10:10 *"The thief comes only to steal and kill and destroy; I have come that they may have life, and have it to the full."* When he says "they," that includes you!

Satan is on an all-out attack to steal your joy through your unhappy experiences.

I can't tell you how many times that I have been in a fairly good mood, and then my joy evaporated into thin air by dwelling on something in particular. Before I know it, I'm downright bummed and blue, and I did it to myself. Sort of. Satan started it by whispering his negative, unwelcome thoughts into my head. I just ran with it.

This morning, I sat with my Bible and my iPad and realized how many hours of joy he had stolen from me – all of the hours that I had let him take. I just sat there and listened to all the "woe is me's" and "why not's" and "it's not fair" thoughts that he was gushing into my brain and heart.

My glad easily turned into sad.

I'm so glad we have a rock to stand on. If we had built our home on sinking sand, we would be in extra double trouble. You and I have clung to that rock so many times. Every time we turn around to grab onto it, we are reminded of who we are in Christ. We are reminded of where we have come from, and how blessed we really are. We are reminded about how loved we are, and how He listens to us and values us. These are completely contradictory thoughts than the ones that Satan spews into our ears.

Spiritual battles are very real. You and I have lived them. We have felt them. I know that we cannot be complacent about having our armor on or being aware of what is going on within us and around us. Joy is not something that our enemies want us to live with.

However, we can live joyful lives even in the midst of not-so-perfect situations. We can reject the whispers and the times we are tempted to dwell on those things that bring us down or pull us away from what is positive in our lives. We must keep our focus on Jesus.

When things aren't quite right, we can still tilt our head upward and smile – knowing that the One who has it all in His capable hands will walk with us through every circumstance.

I don't want to be a victim to Satan's attacks or his tricks. I don't want to be an easy target for him to steal joy or happiness from my heart, my life, or my face.

It may be a fight at times, but I'm in it to win it… and I KNOW YOU ARE AS WELL!

Satan, you will not steal my joy. You will not steal my blessings.

Whether his attack comes in the form of a surge of despair or just an annoying, rock-in-the-shoe irritation, he's not going to let you keep your joy without a fight.

If joy was a guaranteed by-product of salvation, then every believer would be rejoicing all the time. But that's not the case. So where does that leave us? We are left with the obvious (and Biblical) conclusion that a disposition of joy must be cultivated and clung to, in spite of every attempt of the enemy to snatch it away.

You know that your joy is rooted in Jesus. He is the continual source of our joy. John 15:11 says, *I have told you these things so that you will be filled with my joy. Yes, your joy will overflow!*

John 16:24 *Until now you have asked for nothing in My name; ask and you will receive, so that your joy may be made full.*

Right now, establish once and for all that He is aware of and controls the details of your life, including the situation you are in now. Your joy is not dependent upon circumstances — it's dependent upon Him. He never fails!

Once that issue is settled, Satan will have a hard time discouraging you, no matter what comes your way.

Along with Paul and Silas who sang in the dungeon and Daniel who stood eyeball to eyeball with the lions, you have learned that God is with you no matter what.

Tell the enemy so! Let him know that if he thinks he can steal your joy by trotting out trials, he can think again. We are Victors today! The problems and frustrations of today are past. Today, tears will be wiped away, and you will have joy - real, deep-seated, all-encompassing joy!

Hold Tightly to Your Joy

PRAYER POINT

Dear Heavenly Father,

I know I sometimes struggle with fear. The enemy speaks lies and threats of "what-if," baiting me into a mind battle. I lay my fears at Your feet. Please give me courage, increase my faith, and help me to truly trust in You. I am asking to be filled with Your joy!

Thank you Lord, that You have given to me Your overcoming power, Your extravagant love, and the supernatural wisdom and insight to see things from Your perspective. Let me be strengthened by Your unspeakable joy.

In Jesus' name,

Amen.

> Who else has dropped their iPad on their face while lying in bed reading Facebook?

 ## JOY OF THE LORD

Lost your joy?

Perhaps you relate to this story: There was a woman who lost her car keys and went tearing through her house looking everywhere for her keys. She opened every drawer and looked under every pile. Finally, she looked in her purse, and there they were! Do you know why she didn't find them at first? She was looking in the wrong place.

There is one thing that I know about you: you want joy in your life. Don't deny it. You do! You want joy in your life. We all do.

But the reason so many people don't have joy is that they are looking for joy in the wrong place. Joy is not a nicety in the Christian life; it is an absolute necessity. A Christian without joy is a contradiction in terms. If you are right with God, you ought to have a continual, conspicuous, contagious joy. I want us to consider how to have fullness of joy.

1. On a scale of 1-10, how would you rate the amount of joy you have in your life right now?
2. Where are some places you have looked for joy?
3. If you could change one thing in your life in order to find joy, what do you think it would be?

Here are a few joy stealers that you might find in your life:

Wrong priorities can rob you of joy. How reasonable it seems to wholeheartedly throw yourself into education, a career, or the pursuit of pleasure! But Jesus wants to be first in our lives, and we will never really abide in His joy until that is the case. Without Jesus, you have no future. He sees into your future and makes a way for you. Put God and your relationship with Him as number one in your life goals.

Worry is another joy stealer. Upcoming events, financial woes, a strained relationship, a frustrating job search - all of us can find things in life to worry about as we experience bitterness. But what do you gain from fretting? Has worry ever changed anything in your life except give you a sick stomach? Paul encouraged the Philippians to cast all their cares upon Christ, and guess what? It still works!

Pursuit of material things is the trend of the day, and one that is so destructive of joy. Stores filled with the latest gimmicks and gadgets offer you just the thing to (temporarily) lift your spirit, satisfy your ego, and gratify your senses. But a focus on these will create a spirit of discontent. Watch out!

Besides watching out for joy stealers when you are experiencing bitterness, there are steps you can take to cultivate joy in your life.

1. Start by deciding to be joyful. James wrote to the early church: *Consider it pure joy, my brothers and sisters, whenever you face trials of many kinds,* James 1:2. He wasn't saying life was going to be peaceful and pain-free. Rather, he was challenging believers to be filled with joy because of the good growth and character that would be developed in their lives.

2. Take time with God. The Psalmist learned it, and so can you: *You make known to me the path of life; you will fill me with joy in your presence, with eternal pleasures at your right hand* Psalm 16:11. There is real joy to be found in the Presence of the Lord.

3. Invest yourself in others. Jesus gave Himself unselfishly to those around Him. We will find Christ's joy in blessing and serving others.

4. Don't dwell on your past failures. You can be sure it isn't God who haunts your mind with the mistake of the past. He loves you, and He's committed to helping you succeed.

PRAYER POINT

Lord, sometimes I just want to give up. My burdens are overwhelming. I don't seem to ever catch up. I can't seem to get started. I feel the pain of stress, hurt and setbacks.

Strengthen me to stand up knowing you are always with me. Fall fresh on me today so I can find my joy and peace again. Restore the broken places in my life. I want to have the resources and love required to provide for me and for my family. I desire the energy and motivation to perform both my job and daily tasks at home.

Give me a fresh breeze of joy to lighten my load.

Send the right people in my life to be a source of love, guidance and new opportunities.

Thank You Lord for Your mercy and grace. Thank You for favor in this season.

I thank You now in advance because I believe You are an awesome God.

I stand on Your promises as You cover me with Your protection and provision. My trust in You Lord allows me to exhale the stress, worry and shame.

Holy Spirit, I am encouraged now and will press on in the name of Jesus.

Amen

> You know it's going to be a long day when you yell seriously at your alarm clock.

I LOVE TO LAUGH!

I believe that health and humor are related.

Laughter has helped me through many difficult times in my life. I find even a soft chuckle lifts my spirit. If you are under stress, take a moment and laugh! Go ahead; laugh right now!

I am reading Psalm 126:1 today. *When the Lord turned again the Captivity of Zion, we were like them that dreamed. Then was our mouth filled with laughter.*

It was in the most festive moment of their lives that that they laughed.

Why did they laugh?

Life had changed!

The transformation from bondage to liberty, from banishment to home, and from devastation to restoration, produced exhilarations of feeling that gave natural way to uncontainable laughter. I can imagine them as they laughed and roared and chuckled and even hooted and snorted and guffawed.

In my imagination, I hear them singing and jumping and playing music, and even dancing! They clapped their hands and danced with their feet and bellowed praise to God.

Why shouldn't they? Their captivity in a foreign land was ended. Joy brimmed over into every nerve and muscle. Eyes fired upward, countenances glowed, voices rang out, and laughter pealed forth in mirth.

It was the time to be filled with laughter! No more exile; banishment had been ended; a great dream had come true; they could scarcely believe it was true,

We, like those captive Children of Israel, have been set free, found a home and been restored. Of all people, we should be a community of love and laughter.

Philippians 2:2 *Complete my joy by being of the same mind, having the same love, being in full accord and of one mind.* The truth is, our unity as believers opens the flood-gates for love and joy and laughter to pour into a person, a community, and any situation.

There is a time to laugh!

There is a time to make merry!

Humor and health are related. Laughter may not heal you, but it can make you feel better while you're sick.

Holy laughter is great, if it reflects a change in your life.

Let us embrace rejoicing, even with all its physical and intellectual exhibitions.

Further, my brothers and sisters, rejoice in the Lord! It is no trouble for me to write the same things to you again, and it is a safeguard for you. Philippians 3:1

Rejoice in the Lord always. I will say it again: Rejoice! Philippians 4:4

The Apostle Paul, who had known every height and depth of life's experiences, instructs us to rejoice! Joy is sensible and happiness is rational. Godly laughter is useful.

God gave me a sense of humor. It does good to have a merry heart. I would rather have laughter that everyone can see than to have hidden things that cripple the spirit and dry the bones! Many people (including Christians) are sour and sad in their spirit.

A cheerful heart is good medicine, but a crushed spirit dries up the bones. Proverbs 17:22

I find that it is good to have a jovial laugh. My best and most satisfying chuckles are not the result of someone else's misfortune but that which is given me by my Savior, who has graciously blessed me with the gift of humor. I am far from perfect here, but I do try to see the goodness of life and the natural humor all around me!

I challenge you to ask God for this invaluable blessing. Nurture the Joy of the Lord, joined with humor and glee. Find your best friend in Jesus Christ, and make Him your joy.

PRAYER POINT

As I walk through this life, help me to create more laughter than tears, dispense more cheer than gloom, and spread more joy than despair. Never let me become so indifferent, that I will fail to see the wonders in the eyes of a child, or the twinkle in the eyes of the aged. Never let me forget that I have the privilege to cheer people up and allow them to be happy.

I love to hear You whisper: "When you made My people smile, you made Me smile."

Amen

YOU'RE SO SPECIAL!

You're so special because God loves you. Even with all that we do that is contrary to His will, God still loves us. God still loves you. He wants you to spend time with Him. He longs to hear your voice and speak with you. He has worked out an incredible purpose and destiny for your life. You're SO special!

You're so special because God gave His best for you. God knew that the world needed a way it could get back to Him. Out of His great love for us, He chose to give His best: His own Son (John 3:16). Who in their right mind would give up their own offspring to rescue a bunch of stubborn, disobedient creatures, let alone allow their child to die for them?

Yet God did this, just for us. Just for you. He gave His best just to give you the opportunity for you to choose to come back to Him. He didn't even know if you would comply, and He still chose to give His best for you anyway. You're SO special!

You're so special because God gave His all for you. God sent His only son as a way out for us. There was no other way, and He freely gave His all. Not only did He allow His Son to come and be our deliverer, but He also sent His Holy Spirit to be our comforter and guide (John 14:26). His angels keep watch over us and protect us (Psalm 91:11). He has blessed us to embody the fruit of the spirit and experience those traits that are unique to His kingdom. Everything God has in His possession He has made available to us. All that we have to do is grab hold of what He has offered us. You're SO special!

So today, right now, agree with me that you are special. God has a plan and purpose for your life. Go forward to accomplish His plan for your life, knowing that you are His child and He loves you unconditionally.

No matter what anyone may tell you, YOU ARE SPECIAL. Most important, you are special to God.

HE LOVES YOU SO MUCH!

No matter what you are facing today or what the issues may be, take a few moments out of your day and just reflect on the FACT that in God's eyes...

YOU ARE SPECIAL!!!

Today, keep reminding yourself of your special position with God. You are His prized possession, and all He wants to do is show you His love and give you His all. You're SO special!

Jeremiah 31:3 *The LORD appeared to us in the past, saying: "I have loved you with an everlasting love; I have drawn you with unfailing kindness.*

PRAYER POINT

Lord, I pray for myself and each person in my family and all of my friends, that You will fill our hearts with Your truth of who we really are and how much You love them.

Holy Spirit, help me to understand how loved I am by God. Like Paul, I pray that out of His glorious riches He may strengthen you with power through His Spirit in your inner being, so that Christ may dwell in your hearts through faith. And I pray that You, being rooted and established in love, may have power, together with all the Lord's holy

people, to grasp how wide and long and high and deep is the love of Christ, and to know this love that surpasses knowledge — that you may be filled to the measure of all the fullness of God.
Ephesians 3:17-19 Amen.

> You know that little thing inside your head that keeps you from saying things you shouldn't? ... Yeah, I don't have one of those.

ENJOY LIFE!

Take some time to enjoy life! At times, life has a way of running us over and dictating to us what we need to do. We plan our days only to have life pop up and tell us that we need to change our schedules. We think that we will be able to sit and rest, only to have life point out six more things that we forgot to attend to. Isn't life grand?

I think happiness is a goal all of us can agree on. Let's face it — we all would like to be happy. In fact, if you were to make a list right now of all the things you want in your life, chances are the vast majority of things are on that list just because they will make you happy — or at least you think they'll make you happy.

One of the most effective ways for the devil to steal your current peace and joy is to get you to focus on what you don't have instead of what you do have. I want to encourage you to stop wanting somebody else's life and ENJOY your life. Until you do, you won't even get close to being able to enjoy the life that you have. Believe me, the grass is not greener on the other side.

We need to change our focus. Philippians 4:8 *Finally, brothers and sisters, whatever is true, whatever is noble, whatever is right, whatever is pure, whatever is lovely, whatever is admirable — if anything is excellent or praiseworthy — think about such things.* As we change our focus to those things in our lives that reflect Philippians 4:8, we discover what we do have, and become more content. (Phil 4:12)

By the way, as we roll with the hustle and bustle of life, we still have to take ownership of our lives and take time to enjoy it. Everything doesn't have to be done right now. Some items on the checklist won't wreak havoc if they remain unchecked. It's okay to take a break and just sit and be—for no reason at all.

Like the woman in the Bible who entertained Jesus in her home, many consider themselves to be a "Martha" (Luke 10:38-42). She was so caught up in the details that arose from having Jesus in her house that she missed the revelation that Jesus was in her house! Who needs to arrange meat platters when Jesus is holding court in your living room?

Like her, many of us are often so busy making sure everything is getting done that we sometimes miss out on genuine moments where we could have been ministered to, experienced rest, or had some enjoyment. It is imperative that we listen to the voice of Jesus and recognize when we need to be still. We can't get so caught up in the business of life that we miss out on enjoying life.

Make sure you take some time today to savor the world around you. Keep your eyes and ears open, so you don't miss out on living. We're alive! Let's make sure we enjoy it.

Luke 10:41-42 *"Martha, Martha," the Lord answered, "you are worried and upset about many things, but few things are needed--or indeed only one. Mary has chosen what is better, and it will not be taken away from her."*

PRAYER POINT

Lord, help me to walk in a Holy Spirit filled life. Help me to take time to enjoy life, to be a person full of gratitude.

Help me take time to love, to extend my hand in service to those around me.

Lord, remind me to take time to learn, to be disciplined and accountable.

Help me to ask You to make a difference in the small and big moments of my life.

Lord, help me to keep smiling, to be happy, and to be who You destined me to be.

Lord, fill me with Your Holy spirit so I can create a life of joy, and peace and destiny.

And whatever my challenge, let it be an occasion to deepen my life's purpose in You.

Amen.

> This morning I thought I was getting the most incredibly smooth shave with a blade ever, then I put my glasses back on and took the plastic slide cap off.

Living a Blessed Life

INTRODUCTION

Today would be a great day to speak life over everyone we meet.

Ephesians 4:29 *Do not let any unwholesome talk come out of your mouths, but only what is helpful for building others up according to their needs, that it may benefit those who listen.*

So here's how it works: first you take note that many of the people you meet are like a dirty clay pot on the outside. Then, remind yourself that there is a treasure hidden on the inside, and you and Jesus get to discover that treasure.

Regardless of how we look on the outside, as believers, we are on our way to becoming more and more like Jesus. The Apostle Paul would say that you have *"Christ in you, the hope of glory!"*

When you see someone who is destroying their life, someone who is broken, obnoxious, depressed, deluded, you can literally call the treasure out of them — encourage it right out.

It is there. The problem is many of us are not so well-practiced at seeing it. We need to start looking at people as if we were a loving father or a loving mother, and less like angry siblings.

This isn't just for people who already know Jesus. You know that every person you have ever met was made in the image of God. Everyone! The greatest gift we can give each other is by affirming each other with these words: "You know, you look just like your Father."

"You are your Father's daughter. I can just see Jesus in you when you do that. You are your Father's son."

You can actually say that to people that aren't Christians—those who don't even know Jesus. You can choose to affirm those things that look like Jesus in their lives. You can say things like "You're such a great waiter! Wow—no one has ever served me dinner with that much skill. I just think God loves this about you!"

Those are the words of life. Those are the words of a loving Father. You can make a habit of affirming the treasure in those you meet.

RELIGION VS. RELATIONSHIP

You find that you have followed all the church rules, attended all the services, given in all the offerings and yet, something is missing. Allow me to encourage you with this truth: it's not about keeping a religion. It is about relationship.

In the Word, there are over 50 *one another* verses describing a church that is built on people-to-people dynamics: love one another, accept one another, bear one another's burdens, etc. The type of Christian culture described in Scripture seems to place all of the elements of church life (worship, discipleship, learning, growing, and giving to others) within the context of relationship. For example, you will never find a discipleship program or conference in Scripture, but you will see exhortations for older saints to teach and mentor the younger ones. In other words, within the church family, faith was passed on from one to another in a relationship. WOW!

So how do you know if you have been caught in "religion"?

- When God is a distant concept to you instead of a real presence.

- When you find yourself following another man, woman, or a set of principles instead of following Jesus.

- When fear of eternity, not measuring up, or falling into error drives your actions.

- When you find yourself in empty rituals that do not connect you in a real way to Him.

- When you are burdened by the expectations of others and feel guilty when you can't do enough.

- When you look at others who struggle with contempt instead of compassion.

- When the approval of others means more to you than remaining in the reality of His love.

- When you hesitate to be honest about your doubts or struggles because others will judge you.

- When you think righteousness depends on your efforts instead of His grace working in you.

- When following Him is more about obligation than affection.

- When correcting someone's doctrine is more important than loving them.

- When God seems more present on Sunday morning than He does on Monday.

If you have only known Christianity to be a set of doctrines, rules and rituals, I have great news: Jesus came and died to be the Living Way between you and His Father. Religion deceives us into thinking discipline, commitment and hard work get us a higher rank in Heaven. If you have been worn out by religion, you are not alone. Others are just pretending, afraid they are the only ones too.

My own journey has caused me to value relationships as necessary soil for real spiritual formation as well as growth in all areas of my faith. When I experience vulnerable, real, committed, life-giving relationships, I am in good soil. Even when these relationships cause discomfort because of conflicts and misunderstandings, I am still in good soil. This seems to be, for me, the place where I am able to grow, change, and experience God's work of grace like nowhere else. This has become so obvious to me that I can barely comprehend a Christian life or culture that is

Religion vs. Relationship

not seeking, as a priority, to live out of deepening, growing relationships.

Today's truth is this: life is found in Relationship with Jesus and with HIS people.

PRAYER POINT

Dear Lord,

Help me to understand that following a set of rules is not being a true Christian, it's being a Pharisee! Lord, I want to get past this thing called "religion" and get into a relationship with You, my Savior Jesus. I know that the grace of God is the only thing that gains me righteousness.

Jesus, You are the One who loved me so much that You died for me. The deeper I get into a relationship with You, the more Your love and grace produce the good fruit of the Spirit in my life. Thank You Lord.

Lord, help me to remember that a relationship with Jesus, which only comes from getting to know Him better, should be the pursuit of my life. Set me free from that old list of rules, and let me be transformed through knowing You. I surrender myself daily to You! Amen.

THE POWER OF BLESSING

We can change our world by blessing others! It is a Kingdom truth. Jesus has given us instruction to bless in Luke 6:28: *Bless those who curse you, pray for those who mistreat you.*

The Greek word for "bless" is *eulogeo* which can be summed up as *"to speak well of, praise, extol, celebrate, bless abundantly, cause to prosper, give thanks."* It also means to *"consecrate to God."* A blessing is full of lots of good stuff.

You and I, as sons and daughters of the King, have the privilege to release blessings over:

- ourselves
- loved ones
- enemies (better yet!)
- situations
- institutions
- territories
- nations

In a world where the negative seems so predominant, what kind of change could you affect if you became a serious dispenser of blessing? Positive overwhelms negative and light dispels darkness. Why would we hold back?

If you and I commit today to intentionally release blessings as part of our prayer life and our Christian walk, we will take our place among those world changers who know this secret.

You can bless in scores of ways: a smile, a helping hand, a word of encouragement, a good hot meal. Who can assess the value of such acts? The Word of God is spirit and life (John 6:63). When you bless yourself or anyone else in

The Power of Blessing

the Name of the Lord and in the power of the Holy Spirit, far more than your personal power is put into motion. You come into partnership with God and His power!

The impact of our words amazes me. Proverbs 18:21 says *The tongue has the power of life and death, and those who love it will eat its fruit.* What we say has the power to speak volumes into someone's life in both positive ways or negative ways. The process of getting a person out of a hole created by negative words could be harder than what it took to get them there in the first place. But Holy Spirit empowered words, speaking hope, love and truth can set people free and bring healing to the wounded.

The blessing is such a powerful weapon. It breaks open hardened hearts and walled up places with hope, vision, purpose, and refreshment. We can choose today to bless others and release life!

PRAYER POINT

A Blessing for Encouragement

Today, I pray that you will know the grace and

peace of our Lord Jesus Christ and be totally encouraged by the Holy Spirit. I proclaim that His Holy Spirit will both overshadow and consume you. I pray that you are filled with strength and courage and focus in everything you do today.

I proclaim the blessings of Heaven over you, your family and your ministry.

I declare Colossians 1:11-12 over you, that you are *being strengthened (by God) with all power according to His glorious might so that you may have great endurance and patience, and giving joyful thanks to the Father, who has qualified you to share in the inheritance of His holy people in the kingdom of light.*

Amen

> So when getting off a crowded elevator I turn and look at a person staying on and say, "You're in charge while I'm gone." I love the look on people's faces.

WHAT DO YOU SPEAK?

Recently, a good friend of mine reminded me of the importance of watching what we speak. I was putting myself down a bit to my friend when he replied, "Speak blessings over yourself and others, or else remain quiet."

He's right. Every time we open our mouths, we sow good seeds or bad seeds. If we can't sow good seeds into our lives and the lives of others, then we need to remain silent.

If we kept note of everything we spoke to ourselves and others throughout our day we would quickly see which seeds we're sowing. Proverbs 18:21 says, *The tongue has the power of life and death, and those who love it will eat its fruit.*

We reap what we sow. If we sow negative seeds, they will produce bad fruit in our lives. If we sow positive seeds, they will produce good fruit in our lives. Our words become seeds that take root in our hearts. If we speak and hear words like: "dummy," "stupid," "clumsy," we can begin to believe those words. Their fruit becomes a damaged self-image. If we speak encouragement like, "you did fantastic," "you are so creative," "you are a good friend," it produces fruit that is life-giving.

Matthew 15:11 *What goes into someone's mouth does not defile them, but what comes out of their mouth, that is what defiles them.*

I decided to go on a fast from "junk" thoughts, and cleanse my mouth from "junk" speaking. I wanted to fill my mind and spirit and emotions with healthy thoughts and fill my mouth with healthy words.

This isn't easy, of course. I had gotten sloppy and developed bad habits, mostly in how I addressed myself. I've already failed a few times and I'm not even halfway through the month. But I know it's something I need to continue to do if I want to see God produce a fruitful harvest in my life and use me to bless others.

Hosea 10:12 *Sow righteousness for yourselves, reap the fruit of unfailing love, and break up your unplowed ground; for it is time to seek the LORD, until He comes and showers his righteousness on you.*

Colossians 4:6 *Let your conversation be always full of grace, seasoned with salt, so that you may know how to answer everyone.*

A blessing is not blessing until it is declared. So today, declare a blessing over yourself and others. Speak that blessing in the name of Jesus!

Declare you are blessed with God's supernatural wisdom and receive clear direction for your life. Declare today that you are blessed with creativity, courage, talent and abundance. You are blessed with a strong will, self-control and self-discipline. You are blessed with a great family, good friends, good health, faith, favor and fulfillment.

You are blessed with success, supernatural strength, promotion and divine protection. You are blessed with a compassionate heart and a positive outlook on life. Declare that any curse or negative word that's ever been spoken over you is broken right now in the name of Jesus.

Declare that everything you put your hand to is going to prosper and succeed. Declare it today and every day (Deuteronomy 28:1-14).

PRAYER POINT

In the name of Jesus, I speak out to you, my community and neighborhood, that God loves you and cares for you. I bless you that a spirit of salvation might come upon you, that the Spirit of Truth might reveal Jesus. I bless you that you might prosper in body, soul and spirit and that you might always have enough.

I bless you that your hearts might be softened towards one another and to Jesus. I bless you that you might care for and support one another and that true community might arise in your midst.

In Jesus' name, Amen

> Someone said, "We'll have more fun than a barrel of monkeys." Has anyone ever stopped to think how cranky, if not downright vicious, a barrel full of monkeys would be, especially once released from the barrel?

GENUINE RELATIONSHIPS

Many of us have left a church for various reasons: there was no sense of community, no real caring, too corporate; only to carry much of that with us into the next church we attend. It is totally unintentional.

So here is the deal: *But if we walk in the light, as He is in the light, we have fellowship with one another, and the blood of Jesus, His Son, purifies us from all sin.* 1 John 1:7.

Fellowship comes from the Greek word *koinonia*, which means "to share in common." That kind of fellowship is more than attending a weekly church service or a conference once or twice a year—it is "assimilating" into the body of believers, becoming united in a worshipping, loving, caring and sharing body!

According to the scripture, fellowship is not an optional matter for believers. John is saying, "if we walk in the light,", then we will have fellowship with one another. And the result of this fellowship is that "the blood of Jesus, His Son, purifies us from all sin."

Here is some big news for all of us: koinonia—fellowship—is viewed by the New Testament as a non-optional environment for spiritual growth.

In John 13:34-35, Jesus told His disciples that they were to *"love one another as I have loved you."* Since they had been with Jesus for several years, they knew how He expressed love to them. But others who came to faith in Christ wouldn't have the same opportunity of journeying with Jesus. So the apostles carefully described what this love looks like. Through what are sometimes called the "one *anothers*" of the New Testament, we are given a profile of the ways that we can love one another.

Some examples are:

- Encourage one another (1 Thess. 5:11; Hebrews 3:13; 10:25)

- Admonish/Exhort one another (Colossians 3:16; Romans 15:14)

- Confess your sins to one another (James 5:16)

- Forgive one another (Ephesians 4:32; Colossians 3:13)

- Accept one another (Romans 14:1; 15:7)

- Serve one another (Galatians 5:13; Romans 12:10)

- Build up one another (1 Thess. 5:11)

- Be hospitable to one another (1 Peter 4:9)

As we demonstrate our love to one another in these ways and allow others to express love to us, we are living *koinonia*; expressing mutual interdependence as members of Christ and one another.

Christian meetings, conferences, and ministry schools are important in this regard because they enable us to experience *koinonia* during the meeting in varying degrees. But they also facilitate getting together with other Christians with whom we can build *koinonia*-based friendships.

God's plans and purposes have always centered on relationships. After all, that is what His love is all about. People have always been the centerpiece of God's plan. In Romans 12, Paul uses the example of a Body to explain the relationships we have with one another. A body of believers is built of interconnected parts joined together by diverse and interdependent relationships. One part can't survive very long without the others.

The church is also called the "Family of God." A family is a small group of people who are uniquely connected and related to one another; they have same bloodline and name. God uses this description to show the strength of the bond that ties us together as one in Christ.

The joy of journeying together, with your strengths and my weaknesses; your giftings and mine, is a great way to live!

PRAYER POINT

Father God,

Show me where I have been hiding in tradition and religiosity. Show me where I have accepted worldly traditions without testing them according to Your Word. Show me where I have allowed lifeless religious rules to restrict me, rather than allowing Your love to enable me to live in Your abundant, eternal life. Show me where religiosity has deprived me of a vital, intimate *koinonia* relationship with You and with others.

Deliver me from tradition and religion, so that I may truly know and love You. Let me love and value people like You do.

In Jesus' name,

Amen.

> If Plan "A" doesn't work, the alphabet has 25 more letters. Keep calm.

BLESSING OTHERS

The single most important concern we need to have for our family and friends should be the same primary concern Jesus has for us: we must make it our ultimate goal to help them know and love God with all their heart.

How do we do that? One of the simplest and most powerful ways to help our family and friends know and love God is to speak a blessing over them. The concept of speaking a blessing over someone may seem strange, but it is scriptural. It's an ancient and respected custom dating back to Old Testament times (Genesis 27:27-29). The priest or other official who spoke benedictions over the people of Israel were only supplementing the most basic of blessings - the one given by the father to the children.

The blessing you speak over your friends and family can be words you've chosen, or they can be verses that you've chosen from the Scriptures. Don't worry about getting the words to sound just right, what is most important is asking God to bless them with a love for Him and others throughout their day. You can actually lay your hands on them and proclaim the blessing in person. However, they do not need to be physically present to bless them, for God will honor your blessing whether they are physically present or not.

One Biblical Blessing you can use is found in Numbers 6:22-27. This is the high priestly blessing that the priests were to speak over the nation of Israel. This is a blessing that you can use on a daily basis for your family

"I pray that the LORD will bless and protect (name) , and that He will show (name) Mercy and kindness. May the LORD be good to (name) and give(name) peace."

Other blessings from Scripture that you can pray over family and friends are found in these scriptures:

Jude 24-25

Ephesians 6:23-24

1 Thessalonians 5:23

2 John 1:3

Colossians 3:15-17

Romans 16:24

Hebrews 13:20-21

Romans 15:13

PRAYER POINT

Heavenly Father, I repent of the word curses I have spoken over myself (and over others, my child, my finances, my health, my mind, my spouse, my relationship in You). Please forgive me for speaking these word curses and wipe them away in Jesus' Name.

I am standing on Your Word that You would give me the Keys to the Kingdom, that whatsoever I would bind on earth would be bound in heaven, and whatsoever I would loose on earth would be loosed in heaven.

I loose Your perfect will and answered prayers into my life. I loose Your revelations, plans and purpose to flow freely into my life. I pray that my mind is clear; my heart is open and ready to receive Your truth. I pray that no weapons that are ever formed against me shall prosper.

I trust in You, Lord to release everything to me that will allow me to move forward as a Kingdom person.

Amen.

> I love asking kids what they want to be when they grow because I'm still looking for ideas.

WHEN WE FALL

Today, I pray for new avenues, new paths, and God's best—no matter what! No turning away!

You will never find evidence of God "turning away" from an enemy, a situation, or an unpleasant person. But, He has been known to run. He runs to embrace someone who is distant, has made bad choices, or has found themselves in difficult or degrading circumstances and is seeking a helping hand.

In the parable of the prodigal son (Luke 15: 11-32), Jesus poetically painted the picture of a young man who had made poor decisions. He had run from the safety of his father's home. Turned away from the wisdom of a clean life and loyal relationships. He found himself in a horrible place, filled with regrets, and decided to go home. Although he did not expect to be received back as a son, his father ran to him when he was far off and welcomed him home with great enthusiasm.

I think we can all relate to the son here. We have all done dumb things. Every one of us has wandered from convictions and found ourselves in a pit of despair. When that happens, we need to remember that our Heavenly Father is looking down on us, silently pleading that we would return home.

His forgiveness is real and tangible. His love is everlasting. And, His grace is overpowering.

Although we all feel unworthy of His love (right now, you might be arguing, "but you don't know what I've done") as if you have committed the unpardonable sin,

God is just waiting to pick you up, hold you close, and convince you of His love—He will NOT turn away from you.

Even if you have wandered from the safety and purpose of a loving relationship with God, He is just waiting for you to turn towards him. The Father will run to you. He will take you in His arms and welcome you home, not matter where you have been or where you have drifted.

As a source of encouragement, take a few minutes and read the story of the prodigal son. It is found in Luke 15:11-32. Read it slow enough that you can picture the selfishness of the son (we all struggle with selfishness). Allow yourself to envision him as he made decisions that were fueled by instant gratification without a thought to right and wrong, or the consequences. I believe you might relate to some of his motivations and practices. But, before you finish with the story, picture the Father seeing him…seeing you, far off and running to meet you. As you read about the party thrown in the Son's honor and all of the gifts lauded on him, realize that God desires to do the same for you. Be encouraged. You aren't perfect…none of us are, but God is on your side and just waiting to run to you….with NO TURNING AWAY !

PRAYER POINT

Dear Heavenly Father,

You are God and You are releasing REVIVAL across this land and around this world! Thank You for being bigger than any problem, any challenge that I may face. No matter what calamity may come, I can rest in Your peace.

Thank You for loving me always, even when I have made poor choices and gone my own way. Your forgiveness is without measure and Your grace is outrageous.

Every day, I commit to seek Your presence and Your Word to see and hear what You have to say about any matter. Before I react or pursue the opinions of the world around me, I will ask for Your wisdom and direction.

I pray Ephesians 1:17-19 for myself:

I keep asking that the God of our Lord Jesus Christ, the glorious Father, may give you the Spirit of wisdom and revelation, so that you may know Him better. I pray that the eyes of your heart may be enlightened in order that you may know the hope to which He has called you, the riches of His glorious inheritance in His Holy people, and His incomparably great power for us who believe.

Thank You Holy Spirit for revealing Jesus that I might know Him, His ways, His wisdom and His purposes. Thank You for empowering me to live a Godly life, revealing You to the world through my good choices and loving relationships.

Thank you, Father, that Your love, forgiveness and grace is more than enough for ever circumstance.

In Jesus Name,

Amen

> There went the morning toast–– If I had a cooking show, it would be called Do You Smell Something Burning?

YOU ARE BLESSED!

It's a new day, a new week, and a new chance for you! Today, I want to encourage you to look at your life with new eyes. Look for the Holy Spirit working in whatever issues come your way, find the blessing in the midst of every situation!

Before you complain, find a reason to give God praise. Remember - "greater is He that is in you"! You are blessed! You have another day of life! God is worthy to be praised. Every day you wake up is a new opportunity.

Forget about what happened yesterday. It's over and done with. No matter what your mistakes, no matter what you did, today is a time for you to begin again. He makes all things new.

In order to move forward, you have to look forward. Even if you are dealing with tough issues, you still are able to move forward. It may not be the mile that you wanted... but every inch is new ground covered. Stay encouraged! Keep moving!

I love David's example. During the most difficult time in David's life, he wrote the Book of Psalms. David lived for a time on the run for his life from the king. He also committed adultery and suffered a loss of his infant son due to his sin, and David's family faced much turmoil during the final years of his life.

Yet, as you read the Psalms, in between the lines of David's pain, you discover hope in God. In the midst of his cries for help and rescue, you discover his Deliverer. David found it within himself to remember the Word of the Lord. He chose to remember the greatness and faithfulness of His God. He took courage knowing the Lord was on his side. David was able to find the blessing in his storm.

There are many dark nights when I have found myself being comforted by the Psalms. In my deepest fears, I have found my hope in the Lord. David's words have uniquely expressed my heart to the Lord, and in turn, have told of His love for me.

No matter whatever you are facing, God is still in control. No matter how tough yesterday was, you woke up to a brand new day today. Follow David's example and turn your heart to the Lord. Take a moment to remember the greatness and faithfulness of the God you serve. Look forward with the heart of an overcomer. You are blessed!

PRAYER POINT

Make this Psalm of David your prayer:

Psalm 27:1-8, 13,14

¹The LORD is my light and my salvation —
whom shall I fear?
The LORD is the stronghold of my life —
of whom shall I be afraid?
² When the wicked advance against me
to devour me, it is my enemies and my foes
who will stumble and fall.
³ Though an army besiege me, my heart will not fear;
though war break out against me,
even then I will be confident.

⁴*One thing I ask from the LORD, this only do I seek:*
that I may dwell in the house of the LORD
all the days of my life,
to gaze on the beauty of the LORD and to
seek Him in his temple.
⁵ *For in the day of trouble*
he will keep me safe in his dwelling;
he will hide me in the shelter of his sacred tent
and set me high upon a rock.
⁶ *Then my head will be exalted*
above the enemies who surround me;
at his sacred tent I will sacrifice with shouts of joy;
I will sing and make music to the LORD.
⁷ *Hear my voice when I call, LORD;*
be merciful to me and answer me.
⁸ *My heart says of you, "Seek his face!"*
Your face, LORD, I will seek.
¹³ *I remain confident of this:*
I will see the goodness of the LORD
in the land of the living.
¹⁴ *Wait for the LORD;*
be strong and take heart
and wait for the LORD.

Living Through the Holidays

NEW YEAR'S EVE

Some days move us more than others. New Year's Day finds us hopeful. Last year's chalkboard gets erased and we start with a fresh slate. Valentine's Day arrives and we celebrate romance. Independence Day awakens our tender affection for Lady Liberty, and Veteran's Day warms our hearts for those who have protected her. On Labor Day, we breathe a collective sigh of relief and enjoy some well-deserved rest. At Thanksgiving, we're thankful and joy arrives at Christmas. We honor these holidays with preferential treatment. We gather, we remember, and we celebrate!

But what about the days after "the Day?" What about January 2nd, February 15th, July 5th, or December 26th?

There is just something about the start of the New Year that gives us the feeling of a fresh start and a new beginning. In reality, there is no difference between December 31 and January 1.

Nothing mystical occurs at midnight on December 31. And yet, we look to the new year, as a new beginning; a time to make new resolutions for this new year.

The Bible does not speak for or against the concept of New Year's resolutions. However, if a Christian determines to make a New Year's resolution, what kind of resolution should he or she make?

Here are some suggestions:

- Ask the Lord for wisdom (James 1:5) in regards to what resolutions, if any, He would have you make;

- Pray for wisdom as to how to fulfill the goals God gives you;

- Rely on God's strength to help you;

- Find an accountability partner who will help you and encourage you;

- Don't become discouraged with occasional failures, allow them to motivate you further;

- Rejoice in your successes, but give God the Glory. Psalms 37:5-6 says, *Commit your way to the Lord; trust in Him and He will do this: he will make your righteousness shine like the dawn, the justice of your cause like the noonday sun.*

Most importantly, like Joshua, choose to serve the Lord this year. Joshua 24:14-15 *Now fear the LORD and serve Him with all faithfulness. Throw away the gods your ancestors worshiped beyond the Euphrates River and in Egypt, and serve the LORD. But if serving the LORD seems undesirable to you, then choose for yourselves this day whom you will serve, whether the gods your ancestors served beyond the Euphrates, or the gods of the Amorites, in whose land you are living. But as for me and my household, we will serve the LORD.*

May how we live our lives in our neighborhoods, communities, workplaces and families, draw people to Jesus. Let others see the Light of Christ in us. Philippians 2:14-16 Do everything without complaining or arguing, so that you

New Year's Eve

may become blameless and pure, children of God without fault in a crooked and depraved generation, in which you shine like stars in the universe as you hold out the word of life.

Shine through me, Lord!

PRAYER POINT

Lord, make all things new.

Bring hope alive in my heart.

Cause my spirit to be born again.

Thank You for this new year

and for all the potential it holds.

Come and kindle in me a mighty flame

so that in my time, many will see Your wonders

and live forever to praise Your glorious Name.

Amen

> Dear God, my prayer for the New Year is a fat bank account and a thin body. Please don't mix these up like you did last year.

GROUNDHOG DAY

In the early 1990s, a funny and underappreciated movie came on the scene. Groundhog Day told the story of a self-absorbed news reporter that finds himself stuck in an endless repeat of the same day. Bill Murray is perfect in that role of reporter Phil Connors. Connors is less than thrilled that he has been assigned to cover famous groundhog Punxsutawney Phil's annual peek outside to predict winter's duration. Connors looks into the camera and cynically reports: *This is one time where television really fails to capture the true excitement of a large squirrel predicting the weather.*

What got me thinking about that movie again was the plot line where Phil Connors realizes he is doomed to live the same day over and over and over. The plot is summed up in this article in Wikipedia: For Connors, Groundhog Day begins each morning at 6:00 a.m., with his waking up to the same song, Sonny & Cher's *I Got You Babe*, on his alarm clock radio, but with his (and only his) memories of the "previous" day intact, trapped in a seemingly endless time loop to repeat the same day in the same small town.

Connor has this exchange in the film:

Phil: *"What would you do if you were stuck in one place and every day was exactly the same, and nothing that you did mattered?"*

Ralph: *"That about sums it up for me."*

This brought to mind another famous Bill Murray quote — this time from the movie, Stripes: *"And then depression set in."*

So what is the point of these ramblings? The point is that too many followers of Jesus are stuck in a "Groundhog Day" life of their own. They wake up every day and feel trapped in a repeating pattern of frustrating behavior and then depression sets in. Why is that?

Einstein was once quoted as saying that *"insanity is doing the same thing over and over and expecting different results."* While not conceding I am insane, for years I truthfully did approach my spiritual life the same way every day while somehow expecting different results.

I would make a mistake and I would convince myself that I would never do that again. I was grateful that the consequences were not worse. I was determined to stay far, far away from that sin. Before I knew it, I had forgotten the lesson and was repeating my mistakes. I would awaken each morning to my own version of "Groundhog Day." The Apostle Paul wrote about this very thing (not the groundhog part, but the repeating behavior part) in his letter to the Romans 7:15 *I do not understand what I do. For what I want to do I do not do, but what I hate I do.*

Wow – I can relate to that! A bit later, Paul writes, *I've tried everything and nothing helps. I'm at the end of my rope. Is there no one who can do anything for me?*

That is the real question, and there is a real answer offered by Paul. The answer is that Jesus Christ can and does. He acted to set things right in this life of contradictions where I want to serve God with all my heart and mind, but am pulled by the influence of sin to do something totally different.

So what can you do to get out of this sin spiral? Nothing. But wait! Don't let depression set in. This is good news. You and I can't do it. I am incapable in my own strength to escape my spiritual Groundhog Day. Only Jesus can enable me to escape this endless loop of frustration. Further advice from Paul follows in chapter 8 of his amazing letter to the Romans: *But if God Himself has taken up residence in your life, you can hardly be thinking more of yourself than of Him.*

Allow the truth of that verse to soak in.

Do you want to get out of your Groundhog Day existence? Many people realize they can't deal with being separated from God by their sin on their own. We needed Jesus. So why do we think we can deal with our ongoing sin issues on our own? When the Father looks at me on my very worst day, this is what He sees: Jesus.

That is step one. I don't have to clean up my sin to please God. He loves me already because of Jesus. The next step is to learn daily to recognize that the Spirit of God has taken up residence in my life. I am learning that I am the one who limits His power by restricting access and control to my thoughts and actions. I am learning that I don't need to wake up to the frustrating effects of repeated self-effort. I can wake up trusting God, trusting that Jesus has my sin covered and trusting that the Spirit of God will allow me to resolve that sin. Trusting God and what His Word says to be true allows me to escape the Groundhog Day syndrome. Instead, I have a new day full of possibilities to thank God for His amazing grace.

PRAYER POINT

Lord, we don't know how long we will have to wait for an awakening of a "spiritual spring" but let it come!

Lord, bring freshness and a day of new beginnings for us. Bring life and growth and joy and faith and fruitfulness.

We admit it – we are tired of the winter in our souls.

Refresh us now.

Lord, You are Spring itself. Come.

Return, and bring Your gifts of rebirth and life again!

In Jesus' name,

Amen.

> Let's get an extended weather forecast from a jittery, inconsistent, reddish-brown rodent.

VALENTINE'S DAY

Each Valentine's Day, many husbands start to feel our palms sweat with the pressure of living up to the high expectations this holiday brings. While the guys are out there trying to conjure up a romantic evening, many gals are trying to wow their men by measuring up to models. Valentine's Day can bring out many of our insecurities while setting high standards for our spouses.

Whether it's Valentine's Day or not, many of us are walking around with our emotional tin cups outstretched like beggars on the street corner, waiting for our husbands or wives to fill them with security and significance. However, the reality is that our spouses were never meant to fill our emotional tin cups—only God can.

When we expect our spouses to meet all of our needs we inadvertently put them on a throne in our heart that was designed only for our Lord, we will be greatly disappointed. We can change all of that. Every day, give your spouse the gift of a relationship centered in God's love.

A relationship centered in God's love acknowledges that the Lord is your personal source of significance, security and satisfaction. When I turn to the Lord in my neediness to hear Him say to me, *The king is enthralled by your beauty; honor Him, for he is your Lord* (Psalm 45:11), then I can let my spouse off the hook as to whether he/she makes me feel secure about myself.

When I seek God because *You make known to me the path of life; you will fill me with joy in your presence, with eternal pleasures at your right hand* (Psalm 16:11), then God can touch the secret places of my heart that no person ever could reach to give me the fulfillment my soul desires.

Valentine's Day

When I remember that my Lord thinks about me more times than there is sand in the sea (Psalm 139:17-18), that He has seen every tear I cried in secret and collected them in a bottle (Psalm 56:8) and that He has counted every hair on my head (Matthew 10:30), then I am wrapped in His cherishing love.

Understanding the truth that God tends to every detail of my life gives me a place of significance that no other person can give or take away. Letting God fill that place in your life instead of expecting your spouse to fill it is a gift to both of you!

Instead of ramping up expectations for love and romance from your spouse, you could celebrate the love God has lavished on you both. When we are plugged into God's love, His love flows freely into our marriages. As His love spills over, it sparks the fireworks that we all hope for in a great marriage.

> Rabbits jump and they live for 8 years. Dogs run and they live for 15 years. Turtles do nothing and they live for 150 years. Lesson learned.

PRAYER POINT

Heavenly Father,

I want to thank You for the precious gift of love You have given to me. Thank You for blessing me every day with this love, and the power and the strength that I get from You every single day. Without Your love for me I can't be, I can't function, I can't even breathe because I need Your love to sustain me. It's like food and medicine for my soul, Lord.

Please continue to let me feel Your comforting love in my life. Lord, I give myself over to You to perfect in me this gift of love, that I may be able to express it and share it with others. Lord, I have not always been good at this. Forgive me, Lord. Some people are harder to love than others, but I want to be like Your Son Jesus.

Please continue the work You are doing in my heart so my heart will be like Yours.

In Jesus' name I pray, Amen.

> Nothing is more romantic than letting you know that I love you... via a Facebook Status update..

EASTER

Easter - The Epitome of Many Illogical Turns of Events.

People don't just roll away massive unmovable boulders. People don't escape from inescapable tombs. People don't cheat death, and yet one person did. A person unlike any other. A person who claimed to be 100% man, yet 100% God. The math makes no sense.

Easter just makes no sense. In an "enlightened," science-driven world, we need an explanation for everything. We need to prove exactly how many millions of years have passed since the last dinosaur lived on earth. We need to chart every star and galaxy beyond our tiny insignificant rock. We need to understand and analyze why sunsets are so beautiful.

The thing I love about Jesus is that He took all logic and threw it out the window. It made no sense that He could heal the blind and lepers. It made no sense that He could turn five loaves into five thousand or that He could raise Lazarus from the dead.

It makes no sense that He could raise Himself from the dead.

At some point, don't you think that our limited insignificant selves need to concede the ability to explain everything in the universe—from big bangs to eruptions and earthquakes? Do we need to make complete sense of Jesus and who He claimed to be?

If we could make total sense of Jesus...

Would He merely be a man who in just three years impacted and still impacts more people than the rest of humanity stretching across all of time? It makes no sense that an innocent man who befriended and healed and loved like no other should suffer and die alongside thieves.

It makes no sense that if He was indeed who He claimed to be that He wouldn't just fling Himself from that cross and bypass such intolerable torture.

Why on earth would Jesus die for humanity? Why would he die for those who screamed "Crucify Him!," begging the government to trade Him for a murderer. People, who hate the name of Christ, want nothing to do with Him, and who live more devotedly to television and sports and countless other loves.

This is who Jesus died for! He died for you and me!

Easter just does not make any sense.

Yet it's the countless paradoxes represented in the meek and mighty, servant and savior, lion and lamb, God-Man of Jesus Christ that set hopeless humanity free. Our sinful selves put Jesus on a cross; He owed us nothing. But He literally said "to hell with logic."

Fittingly, it's because of the nonsense of Easter that life makes sense. Thousands of years ago, unrelenting illogical love was nailed to a tree and locked within a tomb. But that kind of radical love would be more than a match for a mere boulder.

On Easter, this illogical love, arose in resurrection life and continues to impact us today.

HAPPY RESURRECTION DAY!

PRAYER POINT

Thank you God for allowing me to wake up this beautiful morning and to experience a new day. Help me to make the best of this day, knowing that the blood that You shed already covers my life for this day. Help me to use this day to become the person that You called and ordained me to be.

Help me to understand that Your life, death and resurrection have eternal purpose. Every time a negative thought begins to form in my mind, help me to be grateful that you suffered unbearably, just for me. You suffered so that I did not have to. This means I can give all my worries and cares to You while moving forward at the same time, because of Your resurrection power that brings dead things to life.

I claim Your resurrection power on this day to cover my mind, body and soul, my health, my finances, my family, my friends and each and every area of our lives in Jesus' name. I have all my needs met in Jesus' name. I am healthy in Jesus' name. I am made whole in Jesus' name. I am healed, delivered and set free, because I claim the power of your resurrection for my life daily in Jesus' name.

Help me to remember this as long as I live – that each new day is an opportunity to recognize and claim the power of your resurrection.

Thank You God in advance for all things.

In Jesus' name we pray, Amen.

INDEPENDENCE DAY

The barbecues are ready, the fireworks have been purchased, and the partiers are on their way. It's time to celebrate our nation's freedom once again!

America has been blessed as the longest on-going Constitutional Republic in the history of the world. These blessings are not accidenta—they are blessings of God. This is evident as we look at the turmoil in other nations and contrast that to the stability we see in America. Preserving American liberty depends first upon our understanding of the foundations on which this great country was built, and then it depends on preserving the principles on which it was founded.

On July 2, 1776, Congress voted to approve a complete separation from England. Two days later, the early draft of the Declaration of Independence was signed. Four days later, members of Congress took the document and read it out loud from the steps of Independence Hall, proclaiming it to the city of Philadelphia, and afterwards they rang the Liberty Bell. The inscription on the top of the bell is from Leviticus 25:10, which reads, *Proclaim liberty throughout the land and to all the inhabitants thereof.*

As we celebrate the fact that we are a free country, let's also take some time to rejoice that we are free from the bondage of sin! We don't have to be held captive by the enemy anymore! Any time the devil comes with his suggestions and lies, we have the power to throw him out!

We have the privilege of being seen as righteous in the eyes of God. Because of Jesus' sacrifice, those sins we used to carry are now washed away, and we stand as pure as clean snow in the eyes of God. Amazing!

We do not have to be ashamed, we do not have to bear guilt, we do not have to feel like we are "less than." We are joint heirs with Christ! Once we were outcasts, but now we are called children of God!

So enjoy the cookouts, the laughter, and the fireworks. However, make sure you take some time in the midst of your festivities to thank Jesus for cleansing you from all sin. YOU ARE FREE! John 8:36 *So if the Son sets you free, you will be free indeed. So - today and every day, we can celebrate our freedom!*

Today, we celebrate our country's birthday in freedom. The Fourth of July is a time of celebration - music, family, friends, travel, picnics and fireworks. As we celebrate, we should pause to remember all those who worked so hard and sacrificed so much to make the United States such a great country.

It was on July 2, 1776, that the Second Continental Congress approved a resolution of independence. John Adams wrote to his wife: *It ought to be solemnized with pomp and parade, with shows, games, sports, guns, bells, bonfires, and illuminations, from one end of this continent to the other, from this time forward forever more.*

On this Fourth of July, may our celebration be centered on both the political freedoms we enjoy, and the opportunities those freedoms provide to freely and boldly share the love of Christ with our world. Only in Jesus can anyone be truly free, for only in Jesus are the old enemies of Sin and Satan defeated. If a nation is to be truly free, spiritual freedom must be at the very heart of its efforts. Only then can freedom ring for all.

HAPPY BIRTHDAY AMERICA!

PRAYER POINT

Heavenly Father,

As I and my fellow countrymen celebrate Independence Day and our political freedom, I pray that You would help us to focus on the reality that the only true freedom we have is found in Jesus Christ: the freedom from sin, death, and Satan that Jesus bought for the whole world on the Cross.

Keep me ever mindful that true freedom on earth requires true freedom from the power of sin, death, and Satan in my heart and my life. Only when Jesus sets people free can true freedom truly exist. Help me, and all Your people, everywhere, seek to share that true freedom in Christ with others, for only then can people be "truly free indeed!

Help me to live my life in a way that glorifies You, Lord. Give me the strength to be a blessing in someone else's life today, and grant me the opportunity to lead others into the freedom that can be found in knowing Christ.

In Jesus' precious name I pray.

Amen.

> Just a reminder that fireworks look even more amazing when your not constantly checking your iPhone.

HALLOWEEN

Halloween - It's a time of year when the air gets crisper and the days get shorter. For many of our youngest Americans, the excitement grows in anticipation of the darkest, spookiest holiday of the year. Retailers also rejoice as they warm up their cash registers to receive an average of $79.82 per household in decorations, costumes, candy, and greeting cards. Halloween brings in approximately $8 billion each year.

A sure sign of Autumn is that candy corn and treats, decorative gourds and pumpkins are popping up everywhere in retail stores. Halloween costumes and disguises are selling out in stores as trick-or-treaters are ready to take over the streets. A popular symbol of both harvest time and Halloween is the pumpkin. I was thinking recently that being a Christian is a lot like being a pumpkin.

You Are God's Pumpkin!

Perhaps you are visualizing this orange, round vegetable and wondering how you could ever be compared to one of these squashes! Simply put, like a child chooses a pumpkin to carve an image upon, so God carves and molds His own unique design in you.

The Scriptures tell us that the Lord chooses us. He lifts us up and washes the dirt from our skin. Then he opens us, connecting deep inside to scoop out all the slimy, yucky stuff, including seeds of doubt, spite, lies, and fear. Then He carves a new creation, and makes our faces shine by putting His light inside for all to see.

Sometimes I feel like I don't want my light to shine because I am ashamed of a thought or action or pattern in my life. I try to hide the light Christ has put in me, and blend in with the crowd. What I forget is that when God carved me, created me, and gave me His Son, I no longer had to count on my own strength. I can count on the Lord's. It is He who washes me clean. It is He who gives me a spirit of strength and perseverance. It is He who makes me pure. It is He who frees me from sin, and it is He who gives me hope. When I realize that my part of the equation is to rely on His strength and power, then I can do as Scriptures say and shine His light through the power of the Holy Spirit.

What starts as an everyday squash turns into a lantern of light. What starts as an everyday person turns into a beacon of hope for all to see. Through our union with Christ, we are given the light and wisdom of the Holy Spirit who enters and dwells in our lives. It is He who picked you out and carved you just the way He wants you. Make sure you keep your lantern lit for all to see.

A few thoughts about Halloween...

By the way, there's nothing inherently evil about candy, costumes, or trick-or-treating in the neighborhood. In fact, all of that can provide a unique gospel opportunity with neighbors. Even handing out candy to neighborhood children (provided you're not stingy) can improve your reputation among the kids. Actually, trick-or-treating can be used to further gospel interests.

Ultimately, Christian participation in Halloween is a matter of conscience before God. Whatever level of Halloween participation you choose; you must honor God by showing mercy to those who are perishing. Halloween provides the Christian with the opportunity to accomplish both of those things in the gospel of Jesus Christ; it's a message that is the very mercy of a forgiving God. What better time of the year is there to share such a message than Halloween? Here are a couple verses to read: Psalm 19:7-10; Colossians 2:3.

PRAYER POINT

Father in Heaven,

On this evening, guide little ones, elders, and everyone in-between safely as they cross paths with strangers, knock on neighbor's doors and open their own front doors. And Lord, as I carve my pumpkin, this is my prayer:

Open my mind so I can learn about You; (Cut the top of the pumpkin)

Take away all my sin and forgive me for the wrong things I do. (Clean out the inside)

Open my eyes so Your love I will see; (Cut the eyes out in heart shapes)

I'm so sorry for turning up my nose to all You've given me. (Cut a nose in the shape of a cross)

Open my ears so your word I will hear; (Cut the ears shaped like the Bible — we did rectangles)

Open my mouth so I can tell others You are near; (cut the mouth in a happy smile)

Let Your light shine in all I say and do! (Place a candle inside and light it).

Amen!

> Thank you, Halloween. All of a sudden, cobwebs in my house are decorations.

ELECTION DAY

Every Election Day, I am glad when it is over and I hope the results are in by that evening. I pray that whoever wins, does so by a solid enough number so there will be no disputes, cries of voter fraud, recounts, lawsuits and countersuits. Even though I think the Electoral College is disingenuous, I pray that whoever wins the popular vote also wins the Electoral College vote. I pray for a conflict-free election, regardless of who wins.

I pray for and speak blessings over all those of integrity of all parties, running for office.

I pray there will be no riots and violence after the results of the elections are known. I pray for peace in our streets and neighborhoods.

I pray for our representatives who are running for election or who are presently serving. I pray that after the elections are over, they can come together for the good of our country and work through the difficult issues we face. I pray they will change their paradigm from power to service and from arrogance to humility.

I pray for the Christian church. I pray for healing, and that any divisions or name calling that may have taken place through this election season will be resolved so that the body of Christ will be unified.

I pray for those elected that they will continue to follow their dreams and their passions. If they do not know Christ, I pray they will come to know Him in a real and personal way.

I pray all true followers of Jesus will no longer look to a president or a political party for their security, but to God alone.

I pray for God's will to be done in every election.

I pray that regardless of what happens today, I will accept the outcome as part of God's sovereignty.

I pray for revival in our country, and I pray it will begin with me.

PRAYER POINT

O God, we acknowledge You today as Lord — not only of individuals, but of nations and governments. We thank You for the privilege of being able to organize ourselves politically and of knowing that political loyalty does not have to mean disloyalty to You.

We thank You for Your law, which our Founding Fathers acknowledged and recognized as higher than any human law. We thank You for the opportunity that this election year puts before us, to exercise our solemn duty not only to vote, but to influence countless others to vote, and to vote wisely.

Lord, we pray that Your people may be awakened. Let them realize that while politics is not their salvation, their response to You requires that they be politically active. Awaken Your people to know that they are not called to be fleeing the world, but rather a community of faith transforming the world.

Awaken them that the same hands lifted up to You in prayer are the hands that pull the lever in the voting booth; that the same eyes that read Your Word are the eyes that read the names on the ballot, and that they do not cease to be Christians when they enter the voting booth.

Awaken Your people to a commitment to justice, to the sanctity of marriage and the family, to the dignity of each individual human life, and to the truth that human rights begin when human lives begin, and not one moment later.

Lord, we rejoice today that we are citizens of Your kingdom. May that make us all the more committed to being faithful citizens on earth.

We ask this through Jesus Christ, our Lord.

Amen.

> How come we choose from just two people to run for president and 50 for Miss America?

THANKSGIVING DAY

Before we break out our Christmas decorations and holiday songs, we need to take some time to remember the holiday that comes before Christmas — Thanksgiving Day.

It is important to show our appreciation to the people around us, the blessings we have, and the love that we share. None of us really deserve anything. But the Lord saw fit to bless us with so much. Let's all take some time to stop and show some gratitude.

When Jesus performed a miracle for the ten lepers, only one took the time to come back and thank Him. I'm sure the other nine were grateful to Jesus as well, but it was the one that showed his gratefulness that impressed Jesus. The former leper returned because he realized that Jesus was the Christ, the living God. With this realization, he wasn't only healed - he was made whole.

When you take the time to consider the blessings you have, you can't help but recognize the hand of God on your life. When I think about where I could have been and how my life could be going, I can't help but see the greatness of God's work in my life. How about you?

In those moments when you stop to give praise and thanksgiving, you open yourself up to the Holy Spirit. When your heart is uplifted towards heaven, the Lord can do even greater work on your inner man to release you into your destiny and change you more and more into His image.

God not only brings healing into your area of need, but through thanksgiving, He makes you whole.

So, don't just let this week breeze by! Make sure your days this week are sprinkled with moments of thankful praise!

Luke 17:15-19 *One of them, when he saw he was healed, came back, praising God in a loud voice. He threw himself at Jesus' feet and thanked Him—and he was a Samaritan. Jesus asked, "Were not all ten cleansed? Where are the other nine? Has no one returned to give praise to God except this foreigner?" Then He said to him, "Rise and go; your faith has made you whole."*

PRAYER POINT

A Christian Thanksgiving prayer

Dear Father,

Thanks for being my Father—not just any Father, but a perfect One who loves me. You love me not because I deserve it but because You are good. I ask that You show me how I can reveal to others how they can trust You as their perfect Father.

Thanks for being a Father who loved me so much that You sent Jesus to make a way for my sins to be forgiven and my broken relationship with You to be fixed. I ask that You help others to understand how great a sacrifice Jesus made for them and how much You want them to be in Your family through the work of Jesus on the Cross. Amen

An optimist is a person who starts a new diet on Thanksgiving Day.

CHRISTMAS EVE

Ah, Christmas! It is a time of festive celebration and cheer. It is a time that brings out the best in people, even those who seem to have the hardest of hearts. It is a season when people enjoy a wide array of activity, whether it be baking goodies to eat or going door-to-door singing carols to all the neighbors.

As for me, I enjoy watching the old classic movies such as *It's a Wonderful Life, How the Grinch Stole Christmas,* and even the more recent classic *The Polar Express*. Each of these wonderful classics tell viewers of what Christmas is about and yet, each falls short in telling about the true meaning of Christmas.

For example, in the story of *How the Grinch Stole Christmas*, the Grinch realizes that Christmas did not come in boxes or bags from a store and he thought to himself that perhaps Christmas means a little bit more. Indeed it does!

In *The Polar Express* when the boy gets to select the first gift of Christmas, he chooses a bell from Santa's sleigh. Santa tells the boy that the bell is a wonderful symbol as to the true meaning of Christmas, just as he himself is a symbol of Christmas. Really, a bell?

Neither story gives a picture of the true meaning of Christmas.

So, let's pick up where they leave off.

Christmas is a season of great joy. It is a time of God showing His great love for us. It is a time of healing and renewed strength. Christmas is when we celebrate the birth of the Christ child. God sent His Son, Jesus, into the world to be born. His birth brought great joy to the world. Shepherds, wise men, and angels all shared in the excitement of knowing about this great event. They knew this was no ordinary baby. The prophets had told of His coming hundreds of years before. The star stopped over Bethlehem just to mark the way for those who were looking for this special child.

Christmas reveals a Lord and Savior who did not come in regal robes, wearing a crown and demanding worship. But rather, He came into this world as a helpless baby. He came into this world not to judge its people, but identify with them by experiencing their joys and their sadness, by living their lives and ultimately dying their death.

Christmas is a time of remembrance and for being thankful to a sovereign and righteous God. It is a time to be thankful for the outrageous grace extended to us all by the Father, brought forth by the selfless act of love by the Son, and the unswerving love and guidance imparted to His followers by the Holy Spirit.

Christmas is not only a time for remembering the wondrous Messianic events of the past, but also of those yet to come. *For a child will be born to us, a son will be given to us; And the government will rest on His shoulders; And His name will be called Wonderful Counselor, Mighty God, Eternal Father, Prince of Peace. There will be no end to the increase of His government or of peace, On the throne of David and over his kingdom, To establish it and to uphold it with justice and righteousness From then on and forevermore* (Isaiah 9:6-8).

Be encouraged to share the true meaning of Christmas with others throughout the year, passing on the good news about the ultimate gift of our Father's grace: Jesus.

Celebrate the birth of His Son, Jesus, God's greatest gift to us!

PRAYER POINT

Most Loving Father,

Thank you for this night and for all it represents. Thank You for the hope You bestow, the peace You bring, the love You pour out, and the joy You give.

We praise You most of all for Jesus, Your Word made flesh. May He light our way as the holy star lit the way for the wise men.

Amen

> The year you stop believing in Santa Clause is the year you start getting clothes for Christmas!

CHRISTMAS DAY

John 1:14 *The Word became flesh and made His dwelling among us. We have seen His glory, the glory of the One and Only Son, who came from the Father, full of grace and truth.*

The Word of God is alive. It speaks. When you read it, the Author begins to read you. When God tells us to meditate on His Word, He is inviting us to enter in and discover His glory there. Each word is like a galaxy that you can keep exploring and never come to its end. It is multi-dimensional and ever-expanding in depth and power.

Christmas is the advent of Christ and the unveiling of the most glorious mystery of God's love for us. As we celebrate this awesome event, we can enter into the depths of this wonderful love.

Isaiah 9:6-7 *For to us a Child is born, to us a Son is given, and the government will be on His shoulders. And He will be called Wonderful Counselor, Mighty God, Everlasting Father, Prince of Peace. Of the greatness of His government and peace there will be no end.*

When the Lord says, His name shall be called Prince of Peace, you can enter into that world.

It is like the Lord presents you with a living portrait of His glory and says, "I am the Prince of Peace. Enter in."

What do you seek? A loving Father? Counsel? Security? Direction? Peace? You can find it in Jesus, the Word made flesh.

Enter into the living vibration of His Word and step into that reality. In order to enter into God's living vibration, you need to prepare your heart. How? It is simple.

It is having a childlike heart full of faith and expectation.

It is not complicated—it is much like children whose eyes light up when you mention Santa Claus. They see the Christmas tree and say, "Ahhh." They see the lights and their faces brighten in delight. Their hearts are receptive. How much greater should our response be to the glory of God revealed in Christ, our Savior and Redeemer, born in Bethlehem!

Let us never lose our sense of awe and wonder at the wondrous gift and glorious act of God revealed in Christmas.

So give yourself a gift. Enter into the glory that shone from heaven over the stable that first Christmas night. Meditate on our awesome Savior, and encounter His glory. Jesus is the reason for the season, and He wants you to step in and experience the fullness of all He is and all He has for you and your household.

> Truth is—I prefer not to think before I speak. I like being just as surprised as everyone else by what comes out of my mouth.

PRAYER POINT

Lord Jesus,

As I open gifts this Christmas Day, let me just for a moment, Lord, hold this time in my heart. It is about mysteries and gratitude, unknowing and wrong sizes, snippets of ribbon and screams of delight. Help me to remember the immense love You have for each of us.

With each gift that is opened, no matter how perfect or not, let me feel again the many ways You gift us each day, especially with Your presence in our hearts and the presence of each other in our lives.

Amen.

> I'm not a morning person, but on December 25th, it's a totally different story.

HAPPY BIRTHDAY!

Your birthday is an incredibly special day. I love celebrating my own birthday, and I really love celebrating the birthdays of those I am in relationship with. As a child of the King, a son of God, I want to share why you need to celebrate your birthday:

You are a son of God. Even if you serve a God who is your best friend, you are first and foremost a son of God (and remember that this applies equally to the ladies), for we are all one in Christ (Galatians 3:28).

You are a son because:

1. The Holy Spirit says so: *The Spirit you received does not make you slaves, so that you live in fear again; rather, the Spirit you received brought about your adoption to sonship. And by Him we cry, "Abba, Father"* (Romans 8:15).

    Do you really need more reasons? Come on now! Paul thought that one was enough. In fact, he thought it was so important a truth that he said it twice. *Because you are his sons, God sent the Spirit of His Son into our hearts, the Spirit who calls out, "Abba, Father"* (Galatians 4:6). God Himself calls you His son. He is the one who makes it possible for you to call Him Papa!

2. The Bible says so in many places (Galatians 3:26, Romans 8:14, Hebrews 12:7, 1 John 3:1…and that is just for starters). God wanted to be sure that we understood our relationship with Him.

3. The Old Testament prophets longed for the day when God's people would be called *"sons of God"* (Hosea 1:10). They thought it applied to the Jews

alone, but Paul says it includes even us whom He also called (Romans 9:23). Jesus came to reveal the Father (Matthew 11:27). This is what makes the New Covenant new.

4. *Sonship* is the pinnacle of redemption: not servanthood or friendship. Not even Adam and Eve were identified as sons! Because of Jesus, we have come closer to God than when we started out in the Garden. How awesome is that?

5. We are to be servant-hearted, not servant-minded. Someone with an orphan spirit readily identifies themselves as a servant of God. It sounds noble, but it insults the cross and the Spirit of grace. Servants work for wages but we live under grace and there are no wages under grace. Sons are shareholders, not employees. We don't work because we have to; we work because we are wholly invested in the success of the family business.

Whenever you celebrate your birthday, I bless you with a day filled with hope and love and rejoicing.

Happy Birthday to YOU!

PRAYER POINT

Heavenly Father, Please bless me today, for today is my birthday.

Dear Lord, please protect and guide me as I continue along the path You've chosen for me. Give me the courage to follow in Your light, and feel Your love wherever I go.

Strengthen me to make good decisions in the coming year. Keep me free from illness and sadness, for I am your child. Because of that, I deserve happiness and success in all aspects of life.

We know that life is like a book. With each new chapter, we learn and grow towards what You would have us be.

Bless me now on this day and in my year.

In Your name I pray, Amen.

> A friend never defends a husband who gets his wife an electric skillet for her birthday.

HAPPY ANNIVERSARY!

So today, as my anniversary gift to you, I want to tell you the secret of our marriage success.

Commitment - We are both committed to loving and following God and as a result, we are both committed to loving and serving each other.

We love each other very much, in fact, no one on earth knows me better than my spouse. But, there are times when we get frustrated and angry with each other. Even in the midst of our most heated moments and discussions, the "D-word" isn't even an option so we know that we've got to find a way to work it out. We are committed to God first and to each other second.

Genesis 2:24 *For this reason a man shall leave his father and his mother, and be joined to his wife, and they become one flesh.*

This verse displays the commitment that is necessary to make a marriage work. I will tell you that being committed to God first makes being committed to my spouse easier. I can rest in God knowing that He will give me what I need to glorify Him in my relationship with my spouse. We can truly be joined together in all that we are and do. I can plan for the "us "instead of just the "me."

So remember, feelings of love may come and go. Happiness sometimes fades. But, if we are committed to God first in our marriage and second our spouse, we will bring God glory in all that we do together for Him.

PRAYER POINT

Lord God and Creator, we bless and praise Your name. In the beginning You made man and woman, so that they might enter a communion of life and love. You likewise blessed the union of these wonderful friends, so that they might reflect the union of Christ with His Church: look with kindness on them today. Amid the joys and struggles of their life You have preserved the union between them; renew their marriage covenant, increase Your love in them, and strengthen their bond of peace, so that they may always rejoice in the gift of Your blessing.

Lord, help us to remember when we first met and the strong love that grew between us. To work that love into practical things so nothing can divide us.

We ask for words both kind and loving, and for hearts always ready to ask forgiveness as well as to forgive. Dear Lord, we put our marriage into Your hands.

Amen.

> A wedding anniversary is the celebration of love, trust, partnership, tolerance and tenacity. The order varies for any given year.

Staying Power

April 15th, 2014, my wife Lindy and I will celebrate our 42nd wedding anniversary-- ah yes, we have **"staying power."**

Where has the time gone?

It has been an interesting and wonderful 42 years; sometimes sad, usually happy, often times challenging, but always fulfilling and wonderful !!!

It seems like yesterday when I walked into a high school class in Fresno CA and was immediately drawn to a strikingly beautiful, blond haired, blue eyed young beauty. Over a very short period of time I realized that she was the one for me, and my task was to help her come to the same understanding.

The fact that she said yes when I proposed never ceases to amaze me.

Lindy and I dated for about two years prior to getting married. At the time, I was a Fire Fighter in the US Air Force stationed in Sault Saint Marie Michigan and Lindy lived in Fresno, California.

In the 1970's long-distant phone calls were expensive, so we wrote letters on an almost daily basis.

While unpacking some boxes a few weeks ago, I came upon those letters. We had saved them all; many, many bundles of letters tied together with elastic bands. It is a treasure trove of history, memories and emotions.

As I started to read the letters, the emotions that welled up inside me were almost too much for me to bear. I laughed, I cried, and I remembered.

Happy Anniversary!

The letters were complete with all the love we shared, the loneliness we felt when separated, and the excitement we felt when together.

42 years together - Passing such a milestone is also a reminder of how quickly time passes.

As I was contemplating how remarkable it was to be married for 42 years, I had an opportunity to talk with folks in our fellowship who have been married for 50 and 60 Years.

All of a sudden, 42 years did not seem so long —but still wonderful, each and every day.

People in our fellowship (that together we have pastored for 22 years) have remarked about how Lindy and I are role models and how much our marriage has encouraged others throughout their years...ah yes, staying power!

It really hasn't been that tough, at the beginning of each and Every morning we greet each other with a big hug and three kisses (or more), and before going to sleep each night we do the same

(Needless to say, many more are given throughout the day)

Our relationship is a wonderful thing and is about as close to heaven as I have ever been.

What a great testimony to the staying power of true, Christ centered, love.

Staying power – the ability to sustain relationships and promises over time is becoming a lost art in a world where having a short attention span and being distracted is an epidemic.

Staying power means that you can depend on someone to be there in the future, that decisions will be made with the long view in mind, not just on immediate reward or impulse.

It is possible to stumble into success – but these accidents do not produce lasting results.

The musical world is filled with "One hit wonders" –defined as a person or act that is known only for a single success.

The song titles can be easily remembered, but the artist is quickly forgotten.

Lindy and I have not stumbled into 42 years of wonderful married life; we have been committed to working on it every day and filling it with the Power and Presence of our Lord.

We have in fact made wonderful and memorable music together.

Lindy and Rich — no *one-hit* wonders.

Now we look back and are so thankful. God has been good. We have three wonderful sons who are also married, and we have seven of the cutest grandchildren that God ever made.

We have more friends across the country and around the world then any two people could ever dream of.

We are blessed with a wonderful family fellowship we co-pastored together for 22 years. Yes, Staying power!!

Staying power is fueled by our mutual commitment to the Lord.

Happy Anniversary!

He has been included in every aspect of our lives.

He has celebrated with us in our greatest joys; brought comfort during trials and softened our hearts during conflict.

His love made our love all the richer!

Finally, staying power is about growing together and mutual interdependence. When we share our lives with each other—at home and at work, we develop relationships that make us stronger, individually and collectively. All lasting success in communities, churches, neighborhoods, organizations and families is a byproduct of healthy, Christ centered and committed relationships.

Together we learned to take down emotional barriers, open up and reveal our true selves, and do away with long silences.

We learned to choose to be happy over needing to be right.

We learned how to be good friends.

Most importantly we learned to forgive.

Today we know how to work together and be together.

We know how to give each other space and trust each other.

We know how to have fun, play, and be adventurous together.

We also argue, get mad, forgive and begin again.

When it's difficult, we take it slow. We take a time-out, walk away, get Christ centered, and look to our Heavenly Father for the answers.

Also, when it's difficult, we lean on each other.

You don't have to wait for tomorrow to begin again. Every moment is a clean slate.

And we celebrate in the Lord and in our love and friendship and family and friends A LOT.

Over time, you learn to deal with your own stuff quickly; the other way is too exhausting.

Once you commit to the end, there's a certainty, a knowingness that brings inner peace and peace to the relationship. There is STAYING POWER!!!!

Thanks, honey. It's been a great 42 years... and we have the STAYING POWER to be committed to many more!

I love you MORE NOW than ever, Lindy!

Rich

Made in the USA
San Bernardino, CA
28 May 2016